GOD'S WIS

God's Wisdom for Your Money

JIM DUNN

KINGSWAY PUBLICATIONS
EASTBOURNE

First published 2002

ISBN 0 85476 912 9

Cartoons in text are by Roy Mitchell

Published by
KINGSWAY COMMUNICATIONS LTD
Lottbridge Drove, Eastbourne, BN23 6NT, England.
Email: books@kingsway.co.uk

Book design and production for the publishers by
Bookprint Creative Services, P.O. Box 827, BN21 3YJ, England.
Printed in Great Britain.

Contents

INTRODUCTION

Who Wants to be a Millionaire?

Our obsession with money is growing: how to get it; how to keep it; who's got most of it? 'Dot Com Squillionaires' are the heroes of the hour, heading the Mammon 'super-league' published by the Sunday weeklies. Popular TV game shows and quizzes compete to offer the largest prizes. Books with titles like *Think and Grow Rich* and *Don't Worry, Make Money!* continue to top the bestselling lists. Who wants to be a millionaire? Just about everyone you meet – or so it seems.

But why? Why this widespread preoccupation with money? Does it spring from the mistaken but widely held belief that money is a sure-fire way of getting what you want? Think of some of the things people try to buy with their money – friendship . . . love . . . happiness . . . recognition . . . respect . . . favour.

Or is it because money is seen as a measure of success? 'How much do you reckon he's worth?' is a question that's often quietly asked. Think of the symbols we attach to money. Does he drive a brand new BMW or a beaten-up old banger? Then there's the house – where is it located and what is it like? Is it the kind that has a swimming pool and room for a pony? What kind of holidays do they take? We like to know how much money the other person has because in our society money itself is a symbol of strength, influence and power. Remember the discomfort of a former chancellor of the exchequer when it was disclosed (accidentally of course!) that the limit on his credit card was surprisingly low?

> If a man enters your church wearing an expensive suit, and a street person wearing rags comes in right after him, and you say to the man in the suit, 'Sit here, sir; this is the best seat in the house!' and either ignore the street person or say, 'Better sit here in the back row,' haven't you segregated God's children and proved that you are judges who can't be trusted? (James 2:2–4 *The Message*)

We value people according to our perception of their wealth. Even people with well-defined moral standards and deeply held religious beliefs can sometimes find themselves guilty of this. Knowing someone else's net worth can make us feel envious or disdainful of them. To many people money is the simplest measure of whether you are winning at the game of life. It is, as they say, just another way of keeping the score.

The National Lottery creates, on average, six new millionaires each week, and it's interesting to hear what some of the winners say they'll do with their new-found wealth: 'Buy my wife a new car'; 'Pay off the mortgage'; 'Have the holiday of a lifetime'; 'Make sure that the kids are set up for life'. Imagine having so much money that you didn't have to worry about paying the bills. You could go where your fancy took you; have whatever you wanted; do anything you pleased. It's a nice thought – or is it?

Suppose you found yourself landed with a huge fortune or a large sum of money. What would you do with it? What priorities would put pressure on you? What principles, if any, would guide you? What would be the right thing to do? Poverty may be tough, but at least it's simple; there are fewer options open to you and fewer decisions to make. This does not mean that poverty is OK. Real, genuine poverty is an affront to any civilised society and is an issue that needs to be addressed.

The questions that arise concerning money and wealth are not always economic ones; many of them have deep moral implications: Is it right to be super-rich? Is it wrong to be poor? Should the acquisition and the distribution of wealth be controlled? A leading politician has famously claimed: 'Taxes are immoral . . . they destroy freedom, responsibility, the very bonds of society!' But others have taken the opposite view and made the moral as well as political case for taking *more* of our money to spend on public services. The scope for such debates seems endless.

What are we to make of the much quoted, often misquoted, biblical words, 'The love of money is a root of all kinds of evil' (1 Timothy 6:10)? Few would disagree with this. Many will rush to point out that it is the *love* of money and not money itself that is bad. But is money really such a neutral commodity? We want to make it, hoard it, spend it. We will lie, cheat, steal, take risks, even kill to get it. What is it about money that makes us 'love' it so? Does money have a power of its own?

Beyond economic considerations are the deep moral and spiritual implications, and those who want to live faithfully in this area need to develop their understanding of how money works – not just in the scientific sense of how it flows, accumulates, distributes itself and is best used, but in terms of the impact it can have in the psychological and even spiritual dimensions of their lives. How we acquire it, what we do with it, the attitude we have towards it and the attachments we form with it are all key considerations.

Wealth is a fascinating, controversial and extremely sensitive issue. When our own personal finances are involved, have you noticed how secretive we become? We will talk candidly on occasions about our marriage, our health or our personal problems, but not about our money! What we earn, how much we've got in the bank, how much we give to charitable causes, the cost of our mortgage, the amount of cash we have left over at the end of each month are all things we like to keep to ourselves as far as possible.

'It's not those parts of the Bible I don't understand that bother me. It's those parts that I do understand that bother me.' (Mark Twain)

The Bible, always a controversial and challenging document, has a great deal to say about money and wealth. Indeed, it is much clearer and more straightforward about money than it is about many other issues – a fact that is welcome to some but disturbing to others. Surprisingly, perhaps, Jesus of Nazareth had more to say about money than any other subject apart from the kingdom of God. He gave an unusual amount of time and energy to the whole question of money, and the range of his concern is startling. In the story about the widow's mite (Mark 12:41) we are told that he sat in front of the treasury and watched people putting in their offerings! He saw what they gave and also discerned the spirit in which they gave. He did not glance away as though embarrassed at prying into someone's personal business. He made it a public issue and used the occasion to teach a lesson about giving. From the parable of the rich farmer (Luke 12:16–21), the confrontation with the rich young ruler (Matthew 19:16–24), the story of the shrewd manager (Luke 16:1–12) and so on throughout the Gospel narratives, we discover his views about money. For him, poverty was not always a virtue and wealth was not always a vice. The Bible acknowledges the part that money plays in human affairs and shows that our attitude to it determines, in large measure, how we live in the world.

'If we command our wealth, we shall be rich and free; if our wealth commands us, we are poor indeed.' (Edmund Burke)

No one, anywhere, escapes the power and effects of money. How we feel about our money is central to how we live our lives. It is inextricably linked to the way in which we construct our private worlds – to the way we think, interact with what is going on around us and order our priorities. It is a fact that if we take time to understand the role money has in our own lives we will gain insights, some perhaps uncomfortable, as to who we are in ourselves. It may be that, while exploring some of the issues that emerge, we will even discover things about ourselves we will want to change.

A book like this is likely to be received with a degree of caution as well as enthusiasm. Enthusiasm, because money is such a fundamental part of all our lives and there is great interest in the topic. Caution, because we're almost certain to be wary of anything that smacks of 'guidance' in this area in case it turns out to be just another way someone has of telling us what we should be doing with our money.

But there are lessons to be learned and there is a wisdom that can guide us if we will allow it to do so. Here is an attempt to reflect and channel that age-old wisdom in ways that can be readily adapted to the problems and challenges of everyday living. Starting with how the world of money works and the power that money has, we will progress to looking at the kind of place money has in our lives and touch on practical matters such as balancing the family budget, saving, spending, and giving to others. Beyond this are the deeper, moral considerations: Does it matter who we save with? Should we invest in stocks and shares? What should our financial priorities be?

> Wisdom calls aloud in the street, she raises her voice in the public squares; at the head of the noisy streets she cries out, in the gateways of the city she makes her speech: '. . . If you had responded to my rebuke, I would have poured out my heart to you and made my thoughts known to you.' (Proverbs 1:20–23)

Then there are the wider social concerns like how we care for the poor. If we subsidise poverty, do we simply increase it? We will look at the morality of wealth creation and distribution, the implications of Third World debt, and so on. These are issues that concern all thinking people who have principles they want to stick with concerning their money, not just for the sake of themselves and their families, but also because of the regard they have for their fellow human beings.

This is not a textbook of economic theory. Nor is it a 'do it yourself' guide to managing your money and achieving financial security. It is about the choices that face us, as ordinary people, in relation to the world of money and the kind of decisions, short and longer term, that we may have to make if we are to live equable as well as profitable lives.

What follows is an attempt to unravel the complexities surrounding one of the great social and spiritual taboos of our time so that as we make our way through the moral and economic maze that it represents, we shall be able to find the right path for our feet.

1.
Money Matters

'Money makes the world go round . . .' There is hardly a part of the globe where its influence is not felt. Such is the power of money.

Most of us are wealthier now than we've ever been before, but not noticeably more happy, content or secure. Maybe money is the problem, not the solution; maybe that is what's making us lonelier and more stressed, and causing us to live less meaningful lives. Perhaps the answer would be to get rid of money?

'Yet poverty itself, which only seemed to lack money, if money were gone, it would also decrease and vanish away.' (Sir Thomas More)

Imagine a world without money

This is an idea that has been voiced by writers and thinkers down the centuries. In 1516, Sir Thomas More wrote his account of life on the fictitious island of Utopia, where people lived in happiness because money had been abolished. Plato described a Utopia where, under the beneficent rule of the philosophers, people worked at and received what was appropriate for their station in life.

'Money is a new and terrible form of slavery, and, like the old form of personal slavery, it corrupts both the slave and the slave owner.' (Leo Tolstoy)

The most popular of all money-less Utopias was depicted by the television series *Star Trek*. The originator of the series, Gene Roddenbery, made it clear money no longer needed to exist because the Star Fleet on which the adventurers were 'boldly going' could make almost anything that might be needed. On Earth, most of the problems that beset us in the here and now had been resolved, and the planet had become a paradise for a population of people who were both literate and compassionate. Earth became part of a federation where many worlds, human and otherwise, joined together in the spirit of mutual co-operation.

This is indeed science fiction, but could it ever become science fact? Whatever the view, it has to be said that we're a long way from it! For one thing, it's hard to imagine how a world without money could work unless there was first a profound change in morality. Money was created to remove the uncertainty inherent in trading transactions.

For good or ill, money is here to stay. There is no part of

the human world that is untouched by it. Even isolated tribes, who have no use for money, may still feel the effects of it when, for example, they find their land being taken from under their feet because of the demand for it and the products it yields. To understand how money works, it is first of all necessary to understand what money is.

What is money?

Human beings invented money and only human beings can recognise it when they see it. The rats that ate the stacks of paper stashed under the bed of Sheikh Shakhbut, the deposed ruler of Abu Dhabi, didn't know they were gnawing their way through two million dollars' worth of banknotes! So how is it that we know that this bit of paper is only good for lighting the fire, while this other bit of paper will pay our fuel bill?

Money, as most dictionaries will tell you, is 'any medium of exchange that is widely accepted as payment for goods and services in the settlement of debts'. Money also serves as a standard of value for measuring the relative worth of different goods and services. An alternative to money, in the dictionary sense, is bartering. This involves using commodities like sheep, goats, dried fish, furs, gunpowder, grain and the like. Alongside these commodities are key concepts like 'yours', 'mine', 'let's swap' and 'let's do a fair swap' (value for money). American settlers in the seventeenth century paid for their brides' passage from the Old World to the New at a rate of 100–150 pounds of tobacco per bride!

The Old Testament contains many instances of bartering, the most notorious of which concerns the patriarch Jacob, who managed to persuade his brother Esau to sell him his birthright in exchange for a plate of lentil soup (Genesis 25:29–34). Market forces as well as spiritual forces were at work, with far-reaching consequences!

But bartering is an extremely cumbersome process, and there is a solution. In every language people understand the idea of a symbol: something that can be used to represent another thing that might not actually be present. Enter, money! Objects to be used for money need to be durable and transportable. Gold, silver, lead, copper, iron and bronze have these properties and can be divided into lumps of much the same size. In China, as far back as 1100 BC, miniature bronze shapes were circulating as money.

Coins containing an amount of metal with a value close to that of the coin are called 'commodity money'. But it's heavy to carry, so credit money appeared: pieces of paper on which the institution that issued them promised to pay the bearer a certain amount of commodity money. But paper money wears out. Every day in the UK six tons of banknotes are shredded into fine particles and used as fertiliser! Worse still is the temptation to print more money than the institution (usually a government) can sustain. In 1775 the so-called 'Continental Congress' issued notes called 'Continentals', which it promised to redeem in Spanish silver dollars after the American War of Independence was ended. When the war was over, 240 million dollars' worth of notes were in circulation, but the government had nothing like that amount of silver dollars with which to redeem them. The Continental was worthless!

When a government doesn't have enough reserves of precious metals it can issue fiat money by simply fixing the value the notes represent. This is not the only reason for introducing fiat money. The idea of currency based on bullion was a prey to instant inflation because the intrinsic worth of coins, gold and silver made it tempting for the users to shave slivers of the metal off before passing them on. Thus currencies were easily debased. The pound and the shilling were measures of weight and in order to pay for something costing a shilling you might have to give nine pennies instead of the usual full weight measure of five! It was also a way of hoarding wealth; the best coins were kept and the bad coins used in everyday transactions, thus making it difficult to maintain a permanent standard of value in bullion coinage.

The Gold Standard, introduced by Sir Isaac Newton in the nineteenth century when he was Master of the Mint, made the value of the pound equal to 123.34 grains of gold. It was abandoned by the UK in 1931. The USA followed suit in 1973. By the second half of the twentieth century the world's currencies had become fiat money. With the advent of fiat money, money itself leaves the realm of tangible objects and enters the world of ideas, where there are no limits.

Losing touch with reality

Throughout history money has progressed from the real to the increasingly imagined. To begin with, people traded with each other using objects and actions they each recognised as having a certain value, although the value placed upon the same object or service might, and often did, vary from person to person. With the advent of gold and silver, however, a certain standardising of values came about because these commodities, although relatively useless in themselves, nevertheless represented some very widely held ideas about their value. So, if a government was overthrown or the currency was debased for some reason, the person who had gold and silver had something left that still had value. But when coins and paper notes with little or no intrinsic worth were introduced, the value lay fair and square in the realm of the imaginary.

The next step was to abandon paper and coins and to represent money as numbers on a computer screen or pieces of plastic in our wallets, and with this step we ourselves became increasingly prone to losing touch with reality. Take the case of Nick Leeson, a notorious financial trader, late of Barings Bank:

CASE STUDY

'All the money we dealt with was unreal; abstract numbers which flashed across screens or jumped across the trading pit with a flurry of hands. Our clients made or lost thousands of pounds, we just made a commission. Some dealers in Japan did proprietary trading and risked Barings' own money, but not us in Singapore. We just arbitraged back to back with no risk or filled other people's orders. The real money was in our salaries and bonuses, but even that was a bit artificial; it was paid by telegraphic transfer, and since we lived off expense accounts the numbers in our balances just rolled up. The real, real money was the $100 I bet Danny each day about where the market would close, or the cash we spent on Kinder eggs to muck around with the plastic toys we found inside them.

'I could step forward and with just one wave of the hand buy or sell millions of pounds' worth of stuff. And it was just stuff; it

wasn't bread or milk or something you could use if the world came to an end. My products were notional called Japanese Government Bonds, or futures, or options, but nobody cared what they were. They were just numbers to be bought and sold. It was like trading ether.' (Source: *The Independent*, 7 September 1993)

Twenty-eight-year-old Nick certainly saw money as being unreal. He ran up losses of £827 million, more than the bank's entire capital, and in 1995 Barings Bank, which had been founded in 1762, and was widely regarded as one of the most secure financial institutions around, collapsed under the weight of those same losses.

For people like this, money is an idea and this idea operates according to the meaning they attach to it. Most of the one trillion pounds appearing and disappearing on computer screens across the world each day are the result of currency traders shifting their ideas around. Some of the money represents objects that actually exist, but a lot of it represents objects that do not exist but which are expected to at some time in the future. This is called 'futures trading' and since the future is no more than an idea in our mind, futures trading relates to non-existent commodities or non-existent values for financial products. Some of this activity is carried out to secure a good price for currency in the future and some of it is simply done for profit. This is 'the currency market'. Another former chancellor of the exchequer, Denis Healey, described these changing figures on computer screens as 'an atomic cloud of footloose funds'.

But it is not only rogue traders who can lose touch with reality. Think of some top executives in large multinational companies who, perhaps without meaning to, come to regard company money as their own. The company pays for everything; distinctions about who owns what have a tendency to become blurred, and with this misfeasance comes the added and dangerous prospect of losing touch with one's sense of morality.

Money is power

There are many proverbs and wise sayings that tell about the power of money, reflecting, as they do, the wisdom of the ages and the experience of the masses. Proverbs 18:16 tells us: 'A gift opens the way for the giver and ushers him into the presence of the great.'

CASE STUDY

'I remember as a child having one ability that gave me "wealth"; I could play marbles better than any other kid in the school. Since we always played for "keeps", I could often wipe out another boy's fortune before the noon recess was over. On one occasion I remember taking a huge sack of marbles, throwing them one by one into a muddy drainage ditch, and watching with delight as the other boys scrambled to find them. Through that single experience I began to sense something of the power wealth can give and the manipulative ends to which it can be put.' (Richard J. Foster)

The power of money is legendary. People who control the world's wealth can control the world, or, if not the whole world, then at least the little bit of it that affects them. This produces the seductive thought that if I have enough money I can have the kind of world I want.

There is also a widespread and deeply held belief that money means security. In lots of cases the primary motive for having bank deposits, pension plans and other investments is to safeguard our present and future well-being. 'The wealth of the rich is their fortified city' (Proverbs 10:15).

During the 1970s, when the Rolling Stones were at the height of their fame, it was rumoured that they spent around one million pounds annually on matters to do with their own personal security! It is slightly ironic that the more we possess, the more money we need to guard against its loss. 'Cast but a glance at riches, and they are gone, for they will surely sprout wings and fly off to the sky like an eagle' (Proverbs 23:5).

We try to acquire pieces of paper and numbers on computer screens that tell us we have lots of money, but so many things can spoil our plans. Because of matters entirely outside our control, the amount of goods available for purchase nationally may go down, as in a fuel shortage. Or the amount of money available nationally goes up, causing prices to rise and the value of our money to go down. Inflation bites and what is that but greater insecurity? As a result of events beyond our control, the government may embark on policies that lead to us losing our jobs and, as a consequence, our economic capability. We may look ahead and try to protect ourselves from these calamities by using what money we have to buy more security, but what we actually purchase is the possibility of greater insecurity.

Money is clearly more than just a means of exchange. It possesses a wide variety of meanings and uses within human societies. But beyond any of these there is a factor about money itself which we must grasp if we are truly to understand how it works.

Money is a god

Some people believe that money has a mind of its own. A Palestinian financier said, 'Money is a coward; it will only go where there is security.' Be that as it may, in point of fact money has many of the characteristics of a deity: it gives us security, it can induce guilt, it gives us freedom and power, and it seems to be present everywhere. We attach an importance to it that lies far beyond its worth. Take note, if you will, of the way people scramble frantically for money and of the squabbling there often is as a result:

CASE STUDY

I have an enduring memory of a custom that was common in Glasgow where I lived as a small boy. In those days when a couple got married, the newly weds would wind down the window of their limousine – specially hired for the day – and throw out a handful of coins, usually copper, towards the crowd who stood waving them goodbye. That was the signal for the street urchins, myself among them, to rush madly forward and try to grab as many coins as they could. In the pushing, shoving, scratching mob it was usually the roughest, toughest and strongest who did best.

We would find out where all the weddings were on a Saturday morning and try to be at as many churches as we could so as to benefit from each 'scramble'! Some boys carried blankets and sheets with them, keeping them hidden until the very last moment, then they'd barge in and adroitly catch most of the coins before they'd even struck the pavement.

I have often thought how this unseemly 'scrambling for money' continues into later life. The amounts are, of course, much larger and the methods more sophisticated, but it's still 'a scramble'. (Author)

It's not just the poor and starving who do this. The super-rich, with nothing to gain by having more, still seek it with great energy. Why? This is one of the strange things about money. It is as though it is not willing to rest content along-side the other things we value. It has to have pride of place.

In this century we have witnessed huge efforts to break the power of money by political means, but they have not succeeded. Some countries, like China and Cuba, got rid of money for a while; first as a means of exchange, then after-wards by making it impossible to build up savings. But over time these policies had to be abandoned and money gradually reappeared. This phenomenon is an illustration of what Jacques Ellul called 'the incredible power of money, which survives every trial, every upset, as if a mer-chant mentality has so permeated the world's conscious-ness that there is no longer any possibility of going against it' (*Money and Power*, IVP 1984).

Money is not simply a neutral medium of exchange. It has a life of its own. The teaching of Jesus on money becomes awesome when it is understood in this context. For example, when he says, 'You cannot serve both God and Money' (Matthew 6:24) he is personifying it as though it were a rival god. He is making it clear that money is not an impersonal medium of exchange or something that is morally neutral; it is a power that can dominate us. This is something that we, whether religious or not, desperately want to deny. But our experience proves otherwise and shows that money, whatever its form, has power to win our hearts.

This has enormous implications for us and for the things we will consider in subsequent chapters of this guide. Is it wrong to be rich? Is it right to be poor? Our spending patterns, savings plans, budgeting methods, as well as our giving, are all affected. If our concept of money is that it is impersonal, then we face no moral problems other than making sure that we use it properly. But if we accept the biblical view that money is a power, then our relationship to it becomes all-important.

Money has two sides

Money is a phenomenon that brings into play an enormous potential for good or evil. There is a light and a dark side to most things, and money is no exception. Like the coins and notes by which it is still mostly represented, money has two sides.

The Bible reflects this dual sidedness in its teaching about money, which flows like two great rivers of thought throughout both the Old and New Testaments. There is a positive stream in which the message about money and wealth is decidedly upbeat. Wealth is not shown to be something we should be embarrassed about or even reject. On the contrary, we see that 'Abram had become very wealthy in livestock and in silver and gold' (Genesis 13:2). His son Isaac was so wealthy that 'the Philistines envied him' (Genesis 26:14). Solomon's wealth is legendary, and in the biblical record his great riches are first catalogued in considerable detail then followed by the comment, 'King Solomon was greater in riches and wisdom than all the other kings of the earth' (1 Kings 10:23). None of this is condemned or spoken against. Rather it is recorded in a matter-of-fact way which implies that being wealthy is perfectly acceptable.

Money and what we do with it is even seen as a means of enhancing a person's relationship with God! Zacchaeus, a reformed tax collector, gave his money generously, and Jesus (who did not profit from such largesse) exclaimed, 'Today salvation has come to this house' (Luke 19:9). Wealthy women supported Jesus and his band of disciples (Luke 8:2–3). This support was not refused, but accepted as a much needed contribution. Lydia, a businesswoman, used her status and wealth to benefit the early church (Acts 16:14).

Thus, if we reflect on the Scriptures we will see that wealth is not condemned out of hand. There is a positive dimension that should not be ignored. However, if we continue to reflect, we shall also learn that there is a dark, potentially destructive side that seeks to engage our interest and enlist our co-operation. The warnings about it are repetitious almost to the point of monotony: 'Though your riches increase, do not set your heart on them' (Psalm 62:10); 'Whoever loves money never has money enough; whoever loves wealth is never satisfied with his income' (Ecclesiastes 5:10); 'Do not store up for yourselves treasures on earth' (Matthew 6:19); 'Be on your guard against all kinds of greed' (Luke 12:15); 'Some people, eager for money, have wandered from the faith and pierced themselves with many griefs' (1 Timothy 6:10).

The notion that a power resides within money that is

alien to us and wishes to dominate us may seem bizarre and unreal. In some cases it can lead to the view that the less we have to do with it the better. This is simplistic and naïve, but so also is the view that money is a neutral commodity for us to use as we please. The point is that we cannot escape from money; it is an integral part of human life and society. We must engage with it constructively or be ruled by it; we must conquer it or be conquered by it.

The chief difficulty lies in our being able to distinguish between the two sides, because in practice they are often closely intertwined. If I put £3,000 into an ISA, am I being prudent or selfish? If I give £3,000 of my money away, am I being generous or simply foolish and wasteful? Do my actions and aspirations in the realm of money show that I am using the constructive potential that exists, or am I feeding the negative down side that is always present? Am I using money, or is it using me? To which God am I responding?

These are difficult questions which subsequent chapters of this guide will address. Before reading any further, however, get in touch with your feelings about money. Ask yourself the questions in the table on the following page and tick the boxes. Then look at your answers and ask yourself, 'Why?'

Question	Yes	Not Sure	No
Do I enjoy having money?			
Am I envious of others who have more money than I do?			
Do I want more money?			
Am I afraid of not having money?			
Do I have money I don't need?			
Do I find it difficult to part with money?			
Is money using me?			
Have I got enough money?			

2.
Family Fortunes

This chapter is about income and expenditure, budgeting, and generally performing a responsible financial balancing act – something we all have to do.

During an average working life, a vast amount of money is likely to pass through your hands. Most of us can expect to earn a substantial sum throughout the 40 years or so we spend working. The problem is, earning it over a long period of time is not the same as receiving it up front as a giant lump sum in advance. If that happened you could put it on deposit, earn interest and you may never need to work again!

However, back to reality. It is more likely that this same amount will be dribbled out to you over the whole of your working life and that most of it will be used to cover your ongoing living expenses. It is natural to suppose that the major part of your income will go towards supporting your family, if you have one, and to maintaining a reasonable standard of living, which is of course no bad thing in itself. 'If anyone does not provide for his relatives, and especially for his immediate family, he has denied the faith and is worse than an unbeliever' (1 Timothy 5:8).

'Annual income twenty pounds, annual expenditure nineteen, nineteen and six, result – happiness! Annual income twenty pounds, annual expenditure, twenty pounds, ought and six, result – misery!' (Mr Micawber in *David Copperfield*)

But have you noticed, like Wilkins Micawber (that famed character in one of Charles Dickens' novels), that the weekly or monthly family income and the family expenditure seem to have a way of balancing each other out, give or take a few pounds either way? After paying the bills and taking care of essential living expenses you find, perhaps, that you haven't got much left over at the end of the week or month. In the case of the average person with an average income, this state of affairs can go on for years unless a determined effort is made to alter it.

C. Northcote Parkinson, a prominent British civil servant in the mid-1950s, gave us 'Parkinson's law', which states, 'The time taken to complete a task expands to fill the amount of time available to do it.' Parkinson's law has many variations and one of them is, 'The level of financial expenditure rises to match the amount of income available!' Obviously this kind of observation is made 'tongue in cheek', but there is some truth in it. Unless you focus attention on what is happening with your finances, you may find that cash is flowing out of your hands at roughly the same rate as it is flowing into them.

So, what can we do about this?

Better budgeting

You might argue, quite reasonably, that there's not much you can do about your financial circumstances and that provided you can continue to 'make ends meet' you are doing as well as can be expected. But how will you manage if you run into a bout of difficulties? Suppose your salary suddenly drops or you are made redundant? Circumstances can change without warning and it's hardly sensible to continuously spend every penny you earn without giving some thought to how you will manage if your income is reduced or completely cut off.

Besides spending your money, there are two other things you can do with it: you can save it and you can give it away. Spending, saving and giving are each subjects in themselves, and subsequent chapters are devoted to them, but at this stage it is important to register the principle that good budgeting should enable us to do all three. I hear you protest that it takes all the income you have to meet the daily needs of you and your family; you can't even begin to think about saving, and certainly not giving some of your income away!

Budgeting may sound like the most boring idea ever imagined – a tedious hassle, a totally unnecessary thing to do – but if you do it you will discover it to be a sound practice that pays enormous dividends. Treasure hunts are exciting and so is budgeting, because it is like a search for buried gold! The purpose is to find the money that will enable you first to give, next to save, and lastly to spend – all in proportion to your income.

Budgeting serves several purposes:

1. It enables you to discover exactly what your current income and expenses are. This is perhaps the most important role that budgeting can perform; it will make you more financially aware and that's the first step to being in control. Where money is concerned it is vital that you are in control of it and not the other way round.
2. It enables you to find and reduce the 'black holes' in your spending. The dictionary defines a black hole as 'a region of space where the gravitational pull is so intense that no matter or radiation can escape it'! It's a big empty space that swallows things up and never gives them back. Most people have one or two black holes in their spending habits – areas of the unknown into which their money seems to vanish. It could turn out to be clothes or travel or some other commodity that is quietly absorbing funds. Unless you're very careful, a lot of your money will simply disappear into one of these.
3. Budgeting will enable you to steer clear of debt and tackle a debt crisis effectively. A key aim is to capture some of the money as it comes into your hands and redirect it before it gets spent on the hundred and one items of which you may be only vaguely aware at present.
4. If you keep track of your income and expenses as you go along, you can modify your spending patterns and achieve the goals you've set.

5. It enables your financial priorities to reflect the priorities of your life. Often our finances restrict, or even clash with, the priorities of our lives. For example, a mother who wants to spend time bringing up her children (life priority), but cannot because she must go out to work to supplement the family income (financial priority). Or an elderly couple who want to give support to their unmarried daughter and her child (life priority), but their state pension is their sole income (financial priority). Budgeting can help realign these two sets of priorities.
6. Budgeting, in the early stages, can also reveal certain life priorities that you have. You may always want a better car, a bigger house; you may have 'shopaholic' tendencies you weren't aware of or have ambitions beyond those which current funds allow. Budgeting highlights issues like these and helps you make moral as well as economic judgements about them.

Budgeting is much more than simply recording all the items you spend your money on each month so that you can work out how to balance income against expenditure. It is about finding and freeing up cash that you can use to give and save, as well as spend. The implications of this will vary enormously, depending on whether you are a lone parent with a young family to bring up, a married couple who both work, a single person living alone, a retired couple living on a pension or a married couple who are both out of work. But the underlying principles of budgeting are the same in every case.

Let's look at this in more detail, starting with ways in which income can be used.

1. *Living expenses*: this covers a multitude of items and is where you have most room for manoeuvre.
2. *Taxes (a form of expenditure)*: these have to be paid, but there are perfectly legitimate ways of reducing the amount.
3. *Debt (another form of expenditure)*: this can take several forms, the most common being mortgages and loans. Controlling and reducing debt is very important, and ways of doing this are dealt with later in this guide.
4. *Giving*: this is not something you do because you happen to be religious; it is a principle that affects the whole of humanity. Instinctively we know that it is right to give. Generosity and selflessness are good wholesome attributes. The biblical teaching on tithing (giving away one-tenth of your income) and giving is based on the fact that all we have is given to us by God. There are lots of ways of giving, some good, others questionable. This topic is also dealt with in a separate chapter (see Chapter 4, 'Learning to be Generous').
5. *Saving*: this too is an aspect that raises several moral as well as economic issues and it is one that we must face honestly. How much to save and with whom are questions to be considered. The difference between saving and investing also needs to be understood.

Budgeting for results

The first step is to create a picture for yourself of what is happening to your money now. Use a table like the one that follows (amend the 'ITEM' column to suit your requirements if you need to) and enter all the relevant details covering the last twelve months. If you don't think you need go that far back, do it for the previous six months.

Six-month Budget Table

ITEM	Jan	Feb	Mar	Apr	May	Jun	TOTALS
INCOME							
Salary							
Bonuses							
Interest							
Other							
TOTALS							
EXPENSES							
Food							
Mortgage							
Insurance							
Credit cards							
Travel							
Tax							
Savings							
Giving							
Extras							
TOTALS							

You will need to have all last year's income and expenditure information to hand. If you find this is not possible, use the table to keep a log of income and expenditure for the forthcoming six months. Either way, the aim is to set out your monthly totals of income and expenses so that you can see what the current yearly picture looks like in detail.

Setting out your budget in this way gives you a useful at-a-glance table. The far right-hand column gives you totals for all the different categories of income and expenses over the period under review. The figures along the lowest horizontal row provide a running monthly total that enables you to see quickly which are the heaviest months as far as outgoings are concerned.

Another instant use of the table is the way it enables you to sort out those areas of expense that are fixed, i.e. not likely to change, at least over a six-month period. Things like mortgage, insurance and tax might be included. To bring the budget into line with income you'll have to concentrate on the variable items like extras or travel, where you can perhaps exercise some restraint.

Work in pencil as you'll very likely have to make numerous corrections. Add up the totals and inspect the results. Things to look for are areas where you are not saving or giving, 'black holes' where your cash is simply disappearing, and areas of overspend. The following table is an example.

Six-month Budget Table

ITEM	Jan	Feb	Mar	Apr	May	Jun	TOTALS
INCOME							
Salary	1,550	1,550	1,550	1,550	1,550	1,550	9,300
Bonuses			450			450	900
Interest	15			15			30
Other			100			100	200
TOTALS	**1,565**	**1,550**	**2,100**	**1,565**	**1,550**	**2,100**	**10,430**
EXPENSES							
Food	400	400	400	400	400	400	2,400
Mortgage	250	250	250	250	250	250	1,500
Insurance			300				300
Credit cards	120	120	100	120	120	100	680
Travel	655	30	30	30	30	30	805
Tax	290	290	290	290	290	290	1,740
Savings	0	0	0	0	0	0	0
Giving	0	0	0	0	0	0	0
Extras	200	250	180	260	300	150	1,340
TOTALS	**1,915**	**1,340**	**1,550**	**1,350**	**1,390**	**1,220**	**8,765**

You can add a cash flow table to the bottom to show how your cash is flowing from month to month, like this:

ITEM	Jan	Feb	Mar	Apr	May	Jun
Carried Fwd		– 350	– 140	410	625	785
Income	1,565	1,550	2,100	1,565	1,550	2,100
Expenses	1,915	1,340	1,550	1,350	1,390	1,220
Difference	– 350	210	550	215	160	880
Brought Fwd	– 350	– 140	410	625	785	1,665

From this example you can see that although there is nothing shown in the budget for savings or giving, there is an opportunity to do some of this from March onwards. If there is cash available to do this, then where is it if it's not being given or spent? It's probably sitting in a non-interest bearing account waiting to be used. Jesus tells us: 'Give, and it will be given to you. A good measure, pressed down, shaken together and running over, will be poured into your lap' (Luke 6:38).

Next, you can look to see whether there are any areas of spending where cash seems to be disappearing into the unknown. In the above example there are at least two 'black holes' that are worth a closer look: extras and travel. If extras could be reduced over the six-month period from £1,340 to £1,000, this would release £340 for saving and giving. Additionally, if travel could be cut from £805 to, say, £550, this would provide a further £255, making a total of £595 that could be captured and redirected.

Clearly the figures in your case will differ from those quoted here, but it is nearly always possible to make adjustments of this kind; it's like finding money you didn't know you had! Two more areas in our example might be targeted in the same way: food and credit cards. Budgeting is a challenge in the same way that slimming often is. Cut out the 'between meal' snacks and you'll soon look trimmer; learn to cut out all the frivolous spending, and your finances will soon acquire a leaner, fitter look.

A great advantage of this way of budgeting is being able to watch your cash flow. You can see how your incomings match, or don't match, your outgoings. You can spot the beginnings of a debt crisis. Or you can use the information to plan your way out of debt. A sensible budget is an ideal tool for controlling debt.

Hit the target

You're now ready to take the next step, which is to produce a target budget. To do this, use the same table but this time enter the revised figures to create your target budget for the forthcoming six or twelve months.

Rules for target budgeting

Many would consider it sound advice to pay yourself first. This means taking out of your income an amount for yourself before you even think about your spending requirements. But there is a higher wisdom available to us which instructs us to pay God first. Before spending comes saving; before saving comes giving. When setting your target budget for the year, think of your giving target and put that first.

How much should you give? In the final analysis this has to be a matter for you to decide: 'Each man should give what he has decided in his heart to give, not reluctantly, or under compulsion, for God loves a cheerful giver' (2 Corinthians 9:7). The earliest recorded acts of giving to appear in the Bible are described in the book of Genesis (see Genesis 14:20; 28:22). Someone once said: 'Instead of asking, "How much of my money should I give to God?" ask, "How much money do I need to keep for myself?"' In 2 Corinthians 8:1–5 we read of a church that gave even out of poverty by the grace of God.

A second rule is to avoid setting impossible targets. Once more the analogy with slimming is appropriate. You'll get much better results if you try to make steady progress. If you plan to achieve your financial goals in one fell swoop and then see yourself falling short, you're likely to become discouraged and give up. Be realistic as well as enthusiastic about the targets you want to achieve.

Third, budget to support the priorities of your life. Remember that your budget reflects your moral choices as well as your financial targets. Think carefully about this. Suppose you recognise the need for some extra income if your budget plan is to work. There are basically two ways of achieving this: you can go out and earn the extra money you need, or you can invest some of your savings and let them generate income for you – this is called unearned income.

Take the case of a family who recognise they need some extra income:

CASE STUDY

When Clive and Marjorie got married and set up home they were both working. They established a standard of living based on two incomes and two people living in the house.

Then their first child came along and Marjorie decided to stop work and become a full-time mum. Suddenly they were down to one income and three people in the house, and the maths just didn't work any more.

After a while Marjorie decided to return to work as a full-time teacher, but the pressures started to tell and both parents began to question what they were doing.

There are many pressures on a mother to maintain a paid job:

- finances require extra income;
- a woman has a right and a duty to pursue a career;
- a father has equal responsibility to rear the children;
- the desire to have a life outside the children's world;
- the need for a creative, productive outlet.

If the extra income is important, the job has to be taken and the focus will then be on standard of living. But the choice between this and being at home bringing up the family can be an agonising one to make.

Now consider the case of Ivan, a recently retired accountant:

CASE STUDY

Ivan retired from his job as an accountant and has an annual pension of £15,000. As part of his retirement package he has also received a tax free lump sum of £35,000. Ivan needs to replace his company car with one of his own and estimates this will cost him £15,000. He also wishes to enhance his yearly income and has worked out that the remaining £20,000, invested at 4 per cent, will net him an extra £800 per year.

However, Ivan also wants to extend his house so that his mother can come and live with him. This will take most of his £20,000 capital. But Ivan's church, to which he is very committed, have a building project of their own that would be of huge benefit to the local community; money is scarce and Ivan's £20,000, even if loaned for a period of years, would come in very handy.

What is Ivan to do?

Clearly, Ivan has some thinking to do. As well as economic decisions, he has to make some moral ones too, and the kind of target budget he finally produces will reflect the priorities of his life as well as his financial priorities.

This case study also illustrates the importance of understanding the difference between capital and income. Capital is a lump sum of money, however large or small, that you own over and above what you spend or give as part of your everyday living. Your capital may be in the form of money on deposit (in the case study above, Ivan has £35,000 he can put on deposit) or shares in a company or a home (Ivan has a home, although we don't know how much it's worth, but he may enhance its value by building the extension he is thinking about).

When you have acquired some capital it can act as a valuable cushion to give you flexibility in your budgeting plans (Ivan can use his capital to give himself some extra income). There may be times when you have to use some of your capital to pay for major items such as a wedding or repairs to your house (Ivan needs to buy a car). But remember that if you do this, i.e. reduce your capital, you reduce the amount of income you can expect from it too.

Income is money from a reliable source that you receive

on a regular basis. It can be earned or unearned. But unless you have confidence in the source of the cash, it is wise not to treat payments like bonuses and dividends as if they were permanently guaranteed to continue.

Once you have created your target budget, all that is left to do is monitor what is actually happening on a weekly or monthly basis by comparing actuals with targets. Some people create a third budget table for this purpose and call it a working budget. Others simply leave enough space to write the actual results alongside the target entries. When you begin to compare your giving, saving and spending for each month with what you had budgeted for you will be able to see what adjustments you have to make. Perhaps you will have to go on a cost-cutting drive next month to rein back last month's overspending in a certain area. This is how many companies, large and small, monitor and control their expenditure. Correct variances month by month, or week by week if you must, and you'll quickly be back on target.

There's no need to continue budgeting year after year just for the sake of it. Once you get established and you sense that a 'steady state' is developing, you can leave your budget tables aside and concentrate on other things.

To sum up, budgeting may be a mechanical process, but there are moral implications attached to it. We are more than calculating machines; we are moral beings with choices to make and some of these are about what we do with our money. Two of the key components in any budget are saving and spending, and we'll look at both in detail in the next chapter.

3.
Hey, Big Spender!

Of all the things you can do with your money, spending it has to be one of the easiest and most common. There is, of course, a basic requirement to spend money which all of us have to face, but what if that requirement becomes an uncontrollable urge? What is a proper level of expenditure?

Most of us would agree about the need to spend wisely, but does that prevent us from having the occasional spending spree? What about life's little luxuries? Are they prohibited or can we indulge ourselves from time to time and still claim to be wise spenders?

Then there's the question of debt. The very word sends shivers down the spines of some people. It raises the spectre of embarrassing letters demanding payment, of goods being repossessed, even of homelessness. Isn't the small print that often appears at the bottom of mortgage advertisements intimidating: 'Your home may be at risk if you fail to keep up your payments'?

But is it all bad news? Mightn't there be some circumstances in which it's all right to be in debt; circumstances in which it might even make good sense? Controlling your spending and your levels of debt is key to the task of making sure that money doesn't control you.

Finding the right level

What might an appropriate level of expenditure be? That's a bit like asking, 'How long is a piece of string?' Doesn't it depend on things like circumstances, commitments, current sources and amounts of income? Should everything be judged on a relative basis or are there any 'absolutes' to guide us?

CASE STUDY

Five hundred million pounds – that was the amount of money spent on the G8 summit held in Okinawa, Japan, in July 2000. It was attended by the political leaders of Italy, the United Kingdom, the United States of America, Russia, Japan, Canada, France and Germany, and all I can say is, they ought to be ashamed of themselves. The main topic of discussion was Third World debt!

Oxfam estimated that the amount of money it cost to stage the summit could have paid for the schooling of 12.5 million poor children. The same sum could have freed some countries from debt altogether.

Instead, these world leaders decided to set up a 'Digital Opportunity Taskforce' to share computer technology with the developing world. A spokesman for Christian Aid said, 'For people who can't even read or write and have no fuel and no electricity supply, it's a nonsense.' It's also a matter of priorities, but whose priorities are they?

Clearly, just because something is affordable does not make the expenditure right in a moral or even economic sense. So what might be the cause of such extravagant, unnecessary expenditure? Abraham Maslow spent most of his working life as a lecturer and professor of Psychology at Brandeis University in New York. During that time he developed a theory that human needs are organised on a priority or hierarchical basis. His theory starts with the assumption that everyone has needs that drive them to act, and that these needs have different levels of importance but can be arranged in order, like this:

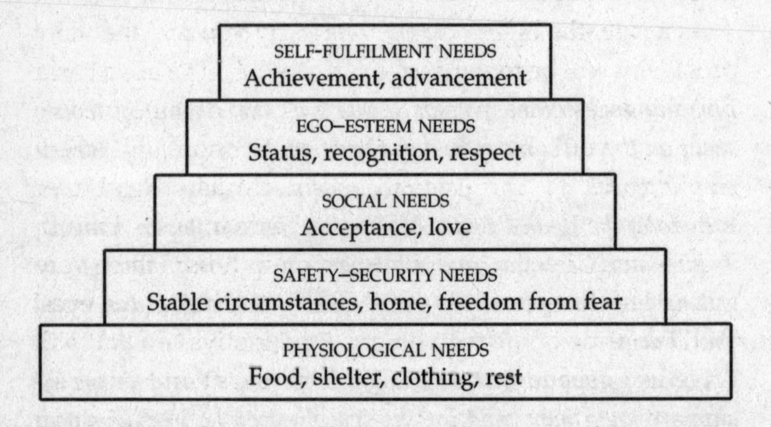

The hierarchy ranges from basic needs at the bottom (like food, shelter, clothing) to higher needs at the top (such as recognition, achievement, respect). Even the disciples of Jesus argued among themselves on one occasion about which of them should be the greatest (Luke 9:46)!

When the basic needs are satisfied, higher needs dominate the behaviour. Maslow's hierarchy of needs goes a considerable way towards explaining why people behave as they do. Money plays a huge part in this because in almost every case we use our money to purchase the things that will meet those needs.

Take another look at Maslow's hierarchy. Which level would you say you were at right now? The lower down you are, the more likely it is that your spending will be on truly essential items. People who are just about managing to buy the food and clothes they need and keep a roof over their heads are not usually extravagant spenders of their money. There are exceptions, however, and you hear sad stories of those with addictive lifestyles, where money spent on gambling, smoking, alcohol and drugs takes priority over obtaining the basic necessities of life.

As a rule, the higher up the hierarchy you are, the more prone you will be to unnecessary spending. The advert in a popular accessories magazine reads: 'How do other people recognise you? By your clothes, your shoes, by every single detail. . .' Extravagance is defined as 'excessive or imprudent expenditure'. The Bible condemns this kind of avarice and offers a way of discerning it. It uses three very telling phrases – 'the lust of the flesh', 'the lust of the eyes' and 'the pride of life' – to describe the motivation that will drive us to spend our money in extravagant and unnecessary ways. 'Everything in the world – the cravings of sinful man, the lust of his eyes and the boasting of what he has and does – comes not from the Father but from the world'

(1 John 2:16). There is a lot to be said for 'godliness with contentment' (see 1 Timothy 6:6–10).

Of course it is important to acknowledge that we have perfectly sound psychological needs as well as material ones. Just because someone likes to drive a nice car, live in a nice house or dress in fashionable clothes does not mean that they have given in to the 'lust of the eyes', or that they are doing these things merely to impress their neighbours. 'Necessary' and 'affordable' have meanings that lie beyond the basic ones we mostly attribute to them.

However, it's worth remembering that 'keeping up appearances', if that's all you're really doing, can prove very expensive. So here is an 'absolute' that could be useful to you: *know what extravagance is and avoid it*. 'Why spend money on what is not bread, and your labour on what does not satisfy?' (Isaiah 55:2).

Don't be a miser!

No matter what your spending level is, it is always possible to spend less, cut back and go without. But adopting a philosophy like this can lead to a loss of perspective, and this in turn may result in a miserly spirit, which is not wholesome. Or it may lead to a fearful spirit through feeling intimidated by your financial circumstances.

Cutting out unnecessary expense can produce grotesque results. Take the case of the mythical 'efficiency expert' who visited the Festival Hall in London and listened to an orchestra rendering a well-known classical work. There are numerous humorous versions of his report. Here is one of them:

CASE STUDY

For considerable periods, the four oboe players had nothing to do. The number should be reduced and the work spread more evenly over the whole of the concert, thus eliminating peaks of activity.

All the twelve violins were playing identical notes: this seems unnecessary duplication. The staff of this section should be drastically cut. If a larger volume of sound is required it should be obtained by electronic apparatus.

Much effort was involved in playing demi-semi-quavers; this seems to be an unnecessary refinement. It is recommended that all notes should be rounded up to the nearest semi-quaver. If this was done it would be possible to use trainees and lower grade operatives more extensively.

There seems to be too much repetition of some musical passages. Scores should be drastically pruned. No useful purpose is served by repeating on the horns a passage that has already been handled by the strings.

It is estimated that if all redundant passages were eliminated, the whole concert time of two hours could be reduced to twenty minutes and there would be no need for an intermission. The conductor agrees generally with these recommendations, but expressed the opinion that there might be some falling off in box-office receipts. In that unlikely event it should be possible to close sections of the auditorium entirely, with a consequential saving of overhead expenses, lighting, attendance, etc.

If the worst came to the worst, the whole thing could be abandoned and the public go to the Albert Hall instead.

This story shows that you can go too far when eliminating what you think is unnecessary! Similar principles apply when eliminating unnecessary expense. The exercise can become counterproductive and can even be detrimental to your well-being. Much better to keep a sense of perspective and let the economic, psychological and moral pressures balance rather than overrule each other.

Here's another 'absolute' you can apply: *eliminating unnecessary expenditure doesn't mean you have to live at subsistence level*. You may stop short at taking a vow of poverty, but try taking a vow of simplicity instead. This is something that has helped many find the right balance.

CASE STUDY

Walter was a retired shopkeeper. He had run a small but successful cobbler business for almost 30 years and was well known and respected by the mining community among whom he'd lived for most of his working life.

He and his wife lived in a comfortable semi-detached house on the outskirts of the town. Both were loyal and committed members of their local church, supporting its work financially and in other practical ways.

The only thing that looked slightly out of place was the shiny new Jaguar that sat in their driveway.

'I've always liked a good car,' Walter explained to me. 'It's the one luxury I allow myself.' Getting to know Walter and his wife as I had done that weekend led me eventually to conclude that the car in his life was not really out of place at all.

Another factor that helps us to set our spending at the right level and to target it at the right things is to consider whether our present spending patterns impair our ability to give to those who may be in need. Sometimes our priority is to survive; at other times it will be to celebrate the goodness of God towards us, and our spending may reflect this. But often our responsibility will be to support others who are in need, and if our current spending priorities stop us from doing that, then we may have to have a rethink: 'If anyone has material possessions and sees his brother in need but has no pity on him, how can the love of God be in him?' (1 John 3:17). This could be another of our spending 'absolutes': *our current spending plans should not overrule our desire or ability to give to those around us who are in need.*

Debt – who needs it?

The idea of being in debt has an uncomfortable feel to it. Running up massive, unmanageable debts is many people's worst nightmare. But we should remind ourselves that not all debt is bad. A moderate amount of debt, properly managed, can be good. A local bank manager once advised me to borrow as much as I could afford, pay it back as slowly as the lender would allow, and hope for a period of roaring inflation in the meantime!

A mortgage is a form of debt, but taking out a mortgage to buy, say, a home, is a wise financial decision. As a matter of principle, taking on debt to fund the purchase of real financial assets, especially in times of inflation, is actually a form of compulsory saving! However, there are certain rules that must be followed.

Don't spend what you haven't got

Although taking on debt can be a useful tool for you to use, if you only have debts and no assets to call on, then if things start to go wrong financially you could find yourself trapped in a situation in which you might lose everything you possess. There are lots of examples of this, such as buying a new car when you have no emergency cash to rely on if your financial circumstances deteriorate. Buying a house and borrowing 95–100 per cent of its value to pay for it, only to see house prices fall and interest rates rise (as happened during the 1990–93 recession), left many people victims of 'negative equity' – the value of their property was worth less than the amount they were borrowing. This situation was made even worse for those who borrowed money to spend on consumer goods using the value of their houses as equity. The Bible instructs us to avoid situations that leave us exposed in this way. Its message is clear: 'Do not be a man who strikes hands in pledge or puts up security for debts; if you lack the means to pay, your very bed will be snatched from under you' (Proverbs 22:26–27).

'Over the past decade, with the recent explosion of credit cards, shop credit and unsecured bank loans, we have become a nation of debtors.' (Bernice Cohen, *The Money Maze*)

Despite such warnings, the debt culture is growing. Temptations to borrow more confront us everywhere. It is far too easy to run up huge shopping bills and defer paying off the loans each month because the credit card companies are often only too willing to increase the total amount of credit you can have. Paying off the minimum amount each month may lull you into believing you are completely in control. In such cases holidays, Christmas and big spending items are routinely bought on credit and the debt habit becomes firmly engrained.

If you pay off the full amount owing at the end of each month, your credit card is a useful budgeting device. You can pay for several items with just one transaction and you get a short period of interest free credit. But if you defer payment and let it roll over to the next month, then, unless you make a deliberate decision about when and how you will pay off what you owe, you have lost control of your account. The credit card company is now in charge and they will monitor your spending to ensure you do not exceed the limits they have set.

Debt that has grown out of control is increasing. Figures published for the UK show an upward trend from 493,000 recorded cases in 1998 to 524,000 cases in 2001. Recent statistics show that debt in Britain has doubled in the last ten years and is now a staggering £115 billion. Excluding mortgage repayments the average household now has around £4,500 of debt. Biggest increases have been on clothing (up by 300 per cent) and telecommunications (up by 2,000 per cent)!

It is estimated that students who leave college or university after completing a three-year course, will find that their debt level is around £10,000. Debts of this size can easily become umanageable. A major high street bank did some research and found that one in every three undergraduates could avoid permanent debt if they had help in managing their money. More than half the students questioned said they could have benefited from more preparation on the financial demands of student life.

Many young people who start a university course will have to learn to live with the idea of building up debt that can only be repaid from income they receive after graduating. Some high street banks offer money management programmes that aim to cut student debt and encourage them to tackle money concerns at an early age, i.e. before they start college. Some companies will, as part of their recruitment package, offer to settle all or a significant proportion of a prospective employee's student debt. The present government is introducing a scheme to attract graduates into teaching, and part of the deal is that student debts will be paid in full, provided those joining the scheme agree to stay in the profession for twelve years.

Keeping debts under control is particularly important for students if they are to build up credit worthiness and be able to raise mortgages in their early twenties, when they want to become home owners. For undergraduates facing the problem of rising debts, budgeting can become a financial life-saver. By keeping detailed records of things like grant cheques, part-time wages and bills for living expenses, students will have a good grasp of their debt situation and be well placed to take remedial action if things look as though they are getting out of hand.

Thankfully, many banks recognise that today's students are tomorrow's wealth creators and are offering good student packages covering things like insurance, overdraft facilities and help with budgeting. Also available is the government funded student loan scheme. Here the rate of interest is index-linked to inflation so that the amount repaid equals the amount borrowed. Repayments can be spread over five to seven years and may be deferred if the graduate's annual income is below 85 per cent of the national average income.

Stay in control

Here are a few of the mistakes made by debt victims:

- They took on too much debt.
- They didn't know enough about their current financial position.
- They didn't budget well enough, or at all.
- They ignored or were unaware of their worsening cash-flow situation.
- They allowed their debt problem to fester.

How do you know when your debts are getting out of control? Is it when the letters demanding payment start arriving from the electricity company, the gas company or the credit card company? Or when your bank manager writes and tells you? Or is it when the bailiffs turn up at your front door one morning?

Thankfully, there are early warning signs. One of them is when you start recycling your debts between your credit cards. Another is when you see from your cash-flow prediction (look at the previous chapter) that the amount by which you are 'in the red' is increasing month by month, i.e. it's not a temporary blip but a definite trend. What should you do in such cases?

Getting out of debt

1. Recognise the problem and tell yourself that it's time to act. Face the fact that your debt has run out of control, and make it your top priority to tackle the problem without delay.
2. Assemble all the facts, even though you may feel you

don't know where to start. You may feel a sense of panic coming over you. You may feel you must do something, like take out another loan to pay the existing ones off. DON'T! Do nothing until you have made a complete assessment of your situation. Get all the key documents together, gather the facts and try to put them in some kind of order.

3. Seek professional advice. Of course, you may be able to see your way forward without doing this, but at least consider it. It's a mark of wisdom and it may help.

CASE STUDY

'The wife of a man from the company of the prophets called out to Elisha, "Your servant my husband is dead, and you know that he revered the Lord. But now his creditor is coming to take my two boys as his slaves."

'Elisha replied to her, "How can I help you? Tell me, what do you have in your house?"

'"Your servant has nothing there at all," she said, "except a little oil."

'Elisha said, "Go round and ask all your neighbours for empty jars. Don't ask for just a few. Then go inside and shut the door behind you and your sons. Pour oil into all the jars, and as each is filled, put it to one side."

'She left him and afterwards shut the door behind her and her sons. They brought the jars to her and she kept pouring. When all the jars were full, she said to her son, "Bring me another one."

'But he replied, "There is not a jar left." Then the oil stopped flowing.

'She went and told the man of God, and he said, "Go, sell

the oil and pay your debts. You and your sons can live on what is left."' (2 Kings 4:1–7)

The greatest source of professional help and advice available is God himself. The woman in the case just described was not the first to seek God during a debt crisis, nor was she the last. Such help is available to us and we must not be afraid to ask for it.

Other help and advice may come through the Citizens' Advice Bureau, debt counselling services, friends with specialist knowledge (and sometimes from those without it!), someone who can help you with your budgeting plans, a doctor (if you're suffering from stress), a minister of religion and even from the company or organisation to whom you are indebted. The aim in all of this is to prepare a plan of action, a series of positive steps that you can take to help you out of your debt crisis.

4. Remember, when you're faced with a debt crisis, the worst thing you can do is nothing, and the next worst thing you can do is panic and act hastily without thinking.

Behold, the tax man cometh!

'Is it right to pay taxes to Caesar or not?' But Jesus . . . said, '. . . Show me the coin used for paying the tax.' They brought him a denarius, and he asked them, 'Whose portrait is this? And whose inscription?'

'Caesar's,' they replied.

Then he said to them, 'Give to Caesar what is Caesar's, and to God what is God's.' (Matthew 22:17–21)

We all have to pay taxes; they are another form of debt. There is nothing new or wrong about this, and in fact it is wrong, both legally and morally, to dodge payment of taxes that are due and owing. This may seem an unnecessary thing to say, but do you remember the infamous 'poll tax', or community charge, which was introduced a few years back and which many people refused to pay because they believed it was unjust? What do we say about those who avoid paying taxes they owe by, for example, not declaring payments made to them?

If we are to pay what we owe, it is helpful to give some attention to the following:

- There are many ways in which you can legally reduce the amount of tax you pay. You should explore these diligently because many people are paying more tax than they need.
- You should claim everything to which you are entitled. There are many tax-deductible items and some of these may be applicable to you.
- You can enhance your giving by making it in the form of Gift Aid. You just sign a form and the amount you would have paid in tax is added to your gift!
- Make the effort to get your tax affairs in order. This includes keeping proper records, for example income and expenditure receipts. It may be worthwhile enlisting the help of a bank or a tax accountant if your tax affairs are complicated.
- Learn about tax matters. You don't need to become a taxation expert – the new look Inland Revenue is making a big effort to become more user-friendly.

4.
Learning to be Generous

This chapter is about two hotly debated topics: saving and giving. Are these two ideas mutually exclusive? Can you be a saver and a giver at the same time, or do most of us have a tendency towards being one or the other?

Saving

Should we have any savings? Is storing up wealth a matter of prudence or pride? Is it a sign of good forward planning or lack of confidence in God?

Spending too much money and being in debt through not having enough are not the only problems people face these days. Many, especially Christians or those with a Christian world view, can sometimes feel a slight twinge of guilt because they *have* money, enough and to spare. The ever widening gap between rich and poor, greater now than it was a hundred years ago, and the poverty and exploitation of so-called Third World countries, makes thoughtful, compassionate souls question whether it's right for them to have savings and investments of their own.

'Gain all you can, save all you can, give all you can.' (John Wesley)

In the previous chapter we noted that a good budget includes making provision for savings to accrue, and there are sound ethical reasons for doing this. Here are a few:

In order to provide for your family

It's worth noting that everyone has a family, even though we may not always be aware of who they are. Michael Caine, the famous British actor, learned quite late in life that he had a brother who was severely mentally handicapped. Caine hadn't known this because the fact had been kept from him. When asked what he was going to do, he replied in a manner typically brusque, 'I'm going to look after him!'

> If anyone does not provide for his relatives, and especially for his immediate family, he has denied the faith and is worse than an unbeliever. (1 Timothy 5:8)

So that you can deploy them in the service of good causes

An Old Testament prophet called Haggai used a vivid

metaphor to describe an unwelcome and undesirable state of affairs. He referred to those who 'earn wages, only to put them in a purse with holes in it' (Haggai 1:6). The money earned does them no good at all. Clearly the flow of money is out of control here, whereas saving money, however small the amount, is a sign of control. Money comes to us so that we might do something positive with it, but if it is continually running through our fingers like grains of sand, then that is surely an issue we must try to address.

> He . . . must work, doing something useful with his own hands, that he might have something to share with those in need. (Ephesians 4:28)

To avoid being a burden to others

This may seem an extraordinary reason, but think about it – most of us save for a pension, whether private or state or both. A further example might be the fulfilment of some divinely inspired personal vocation, mission or charitable purpose. Often your savings can help facilitate this by funding some of the costs involved, or even supporting you as you go about the task.

> Now I am ready to visit you for the third time, and I will not be a burden to you, because what I want is not your possessions but you. After all, children should not have to save up for their parents, but parents for their children. So I will very gladly spend for you everything I have and expend myself as well. (2 Corinthians 12:14–15)

There are numerous worldly-wise reasons for saving, but

most of these militate against the words and teaching of Christ as recorded in the Gospels (Matthew 6:19–21; 19:21; Mark 6:8). He gives the unacceptable reasons for saving as hoarding because of fear of some future event and accumulating wealth just for the sake of possessing it (which amounts to idolatry). The desire to be rich for the sake of riches themselves is forbidden (1 Timothy 6:9). Wealth should be the by-product of what we do, and not the reverse.

There is a tendency among people, even religious people, to confuse covetousness with ambition, hoarding with prudence, and greed with industry. The ancient wisdom of the Scripture helps us preserve the distinction between these, and it is vital that we do so if we are to avoid being sucked into the destructive vortex of greed and idolatry that the love of money so readily generates.

Investing

Saving and investing – what's the difference? Money set aside for future use is money saved. If you stash it under the floorboards of your house or stick it into a vase on your mantelpiece, it will just sit there until you decide to spend it. If you put it into a bank or building society, it will earn interest. This interest can be reinvested to make your capital grow, but if you do that you forfeit the opportunity to take a regular income from it. In other words, you cannot have your cake and eat it! But when you *invest* you can.

Investing means putting a lump sum (capital) into possessions that offer the prospect of increasing the size of your capital and at the same time providing you with a regular return (dividend). The possessions that produce this result are called real assets. You put your cash into a real asset and it produces an income, even while the original sum is growing. Thus, when you invest, you can have your cake and eat it at the same time.

Only a few real assets have this special quality. A house is a good example; a second-hand car or boat is not. Antique furniture, paintings and other collectibles are real assets, but these do not offer capital growth plus income. Most people who want assets that do both, have to rely on stock market investments. These assets are represented by pieces of paper, share certificates or a record on a computer terminal or printout.

Watch where your money goes

Money is power. You can use your money recklessly or responsibly, both as a spender and an investor. Investing is complicated; not only might you be investing unwisely and lose all your money, you could be investing in companies and practices of which you disapprove, without knowing about it.

If you consult any financial adviser about investing your money there are usually four things that will guide them in giving you advice: degree of risk involved, likely returns you might expect, personal circumstances that must be taken into account, and the tax position. It is most unlikely that the ethical status of your investments will come into their calculations. Yet it should, because how a return is made on savings is more important than how much.

Ethical investment

Many 'ethical' funds and shares are coming onto the market now. There are companies through which you can invest that claim only to choose funds that research companies thoroughly and select their investment portfolios based on ethical as well as financial criteria.

Even so, care must still be taken in the choice of 'ethical' funds, as some apply mechanistic criteria to business activities. For instance the Church Commissioners of the Church of England apply a 30 per cent cut-off rule in relation to the ethical content of their investments (e.g. they invest in GEC, whose armaments portfolio is less than 30 per cent), thus diversifying their interest across a number of companies to dilute their 'stewardship' interest in any one firm. But many do not discriminate concerning business methods and this can lead to a policy of selling out in order to get an acceptable return, while ignoring, in the long term, the task of influencing the way in which the funds are managed. Notwithstanding all this, the growth of the ethical investment fund industry is a step in the right direction and offers a more principled alternative to those of us who haven't got the time or the expertise to tackle the 'stewardship' implications of specific shares.

> Recent research by EIRS (the Ethical Investment Research Service) shows that looking only at 15 funds with a 5-year track record, UK ethical funds showed a slightly lower level of risk than non-screened funds over 5 years to June 1998. One of the traditional criticisms of ethically and environmentally responsible funds was that because they invest heavily in small and medium sized firms, they work at the riskier end of the spectrum. This strategy is increasingly gaining in popularity, so watch for it if you are considering changing tack! (Outlook – East Riding Pension Fund, Autumn 2000)

Giving

This is not such a problem to us in terms of ethics – or is it? We like to feel we're being generous – but even that can be an illusion. It's a matter of pride sometimes: we can afford it and it shows we're good-hearted, even though deep down we may not be. Our enthusiasm for the *concept* of giving is not easily translated into deeds or a generous disposition. You can be provoked into a one-off act of generosity by someone rattling a tin under your nose outside a supermarket, or through a cleverly presented mail shot. However, sometimes we struggle to become naturally generous – wanting to give, able to give and big enough to give.

CASE STUDY

A notable miser had the misfortune to fall into a river near his home and was heard screaming for help as he couldn't swim. Passers-by ran to his aid and one man, seeing the unfortunate fellow drifting under a bridge, raced onto it, reached down his hand and yelled, 'Quick, give me your hand!' The miser, despite his plight, drew back instinctively. The request worried him; he had never given anyone anything in his life. There was another bridge further downstream and as the miser floated under it the same man reached down again but this time shouted, 'Here, take my hand!' The miser grabbed it! (Anonymous)

How money affects us determines the sort of person we are at heart. It would be nice to think that our outlook was determined by our faith, but in reality our personal beliefs, convictions and values may have been formed elsewhere.

But let's be fair and practical; there are numerous calls on our pockets – household bills, car bills, birthday and Christmas presents, insurance premiums and big one-off payments like having to replace the washing machine or get the central heating boiler repaired. 'Give what's right, not what's left' may sound good, but it doesn't take account of the feelings of lots of ordinary people whose budgets are already stretched. For them, giving more would mean a change in lifestyle and an unravelling of many existing financial commitments.

'He is no fool who gives what he cannot keep in order to gain what he cannot lose.' (Jim Elliot)

The call to be a giver presents practical difficulties for some people and can lead to strong feelings of guilt. If we are honest it can feel more like a threat to our standard of living than an invitation to experience freedom and growth. We may well feel stuck; tempted not to travel any further down a road to an impossible ideal. But if we do decide to make the journey we have the assurance of a way forward. The encouraging thing about the Gospel narratives of the events of Jesus' ministry is that they introduce us to men and women who responded to the ideal that he taught and became givers (of themselves and their possessions) and lost nothing by it. Quite the contrary, they gained everything. It is true that what we try to keep, we invariably lose, and what we are prepared to give away, we gain (see Matthew 16:25).

If we take the wisdom of the Bible seriously, we must conclude that one of the best things we can do with our money is give it away. It's difficult to find a passage of

Scripture teaching on money that doesn't mention giving. Some Christian writers and thinkers claim that, in the Christian economy, money is made in order to be given away. The main reason for this is that giving is a way of conquering the god Mammon and winning money for Christian uses. Here then are some simple signposts that can help us find the right way forward.

Give proportionately

The Old Testament principle of the tithe, or the giving of a tenth part of one's income (Malachi 3:8), is a starting point. But should this be 10 per cent of the gross amount (before tax) or of the net amount (after tax)? There are several ways of looking at this. Some say, 'It depends on which part of your income you want God to bless!' This is rather trite and perhaps reveals a suspect motive – giving in order to get – which is neither the spirit nor the intention of biblical teaching. Others say, 'You can't give what you haven't got.' After the Inland Revenue have taken their legitimate 'cut', we are able to give proportionately of the remainder. Perhaps this is what is implied in Jesus' statement, 'Give to Caesar what is Caesar's and to God what is God's.' You must decide what is right for you. The point is that giving ought to be in proportion to income.

Proportionate giving need not stop at this. Some have suggested the concept of the graduated tithe. Simply put, this means you decide on a standard of living and give 10 per cent of that amount. Then, for every thousand pounds of additional income, you give 5 per cent more. This way, once you've reached £18,000 above your standard, you are giving away all additional income.

CASE STUDY

John has a business. He has put himself on a salary that gives him a reasonable standard of living. He gives 15 per cent of this salary away. Then he gives away 25 per cent of the profits his company generates above his salary. John also has income from speaking engagements and book royalties; he gives all of this away.

Please don't feel intimidated by these examples. They are merely illustrations of what proportionate giving can mean in an affluent society. Most people will have to take much smaller steps. Some adopt a 'matched-funding' approach, matching pound for pound money spent on, say, eating out with money given to famine relief projects, or money spent on clothes with money given to a relief agency or charity shop.

Maybe none of these is right for you. Maybe you are so restricted money wise that the idea of giving seems totally impossible. But these examples can prompt you to think in new creative ways and perhaps discover something you *can* do in this area.

> Suppose a brother or sister is without clothes and daily food. If one of you says to him, 'Go, I wish you well; keep warm and well fed,' but does nothing about his physical needs, what good is it? (James 2:15–16)

Give responsibly

Our giving should be done in a reasoned way. If we are giving to individuals or organisations, we may need to look into how they will use what we give. What other sources of income do they have? How much will go to the cause we are asked to support? Is it a good cause?

Another way to give responsibly is to make a will. After your lifetime, it will be necessary to sort out what happens to your possessions, and what better way to ensure your property goes to the right people or organisations than by specifying it in your will? If your estate is large enough to exceed the inheritance tax threshold (currently £234,000), some of the amount payable can be avoided through careful planning. It is easy to assume that your possessions are not worth a lot, but this is often untrue. Insurance policies, jewellery, pictures, the home you live in and many other items can all add up to a sizeable sum that may benefit relatives, friends and charities. The following points will help you in drawing up a will.

1. *Get advice.* A solicitor or a professional adviser at your bank can give you advice. The process is simple and will cost you around £100.
2. *Value your estate.* Your solicitor or bank adviser can help estimate the value of your possessions, home and money, subtracting from it anything you owe, such as a mortgage.
3. *Decide who the beneficiaries are.* As well as family and friends you may decide to include causes or charities you support. Remember, a legacy for a charity may reduce the amount of inheritance tax due on an estate.
4. *Appoint executors.* These can be anyone you trust, including those who are to benefit from your will.
5. *Lodge copies of your will.* These should be given to your solicitor or bank manager. Make sure your executor knows where the copies are.

6. *Update your will.* Circumstances change. Make sure your will reflects what you want.

The local church to which we belong is of course a primary vehicle for our giving. There may come a time when it is appropriate to withhold our giving, out of concern for the direction in which things are going, but that should be a last resort. The normal way is to give freely, without need to direct how the church is using the money. This latter point introduces another consideration which helps to balance the notion of responsible giving. There is always the possibility of allowing our giving to become too calculated. Prudent, responsible giving can deteriorate into tightfistedness and the desire to control events. There are times when we need to take risks and give to individuals and groups, not because they have proved they can handle money efficiently, but because they need it.

Give systematically

Sustained systematic giving is much better than haphazard giving. It helps to maintain the 'giving' habit. Planned regular giving also helps those who are dependent on the generosity of others to carry out their own planning and budgeting with a greater degree of certainty. Deliberate premeditated giving sends a signal to yourself, as well as to others, that you are serious about your giving. Of course you don't have to give regularly week by week to be systematic. If you have a plan that specifies how much, to whom, how often and by what means you will give, then this is being systematic. Systematic giving does not mean that the door is closed to spontaneous acts of generosity, but it does mean that you have created a context for your giving and that you are clear about why you are doing it and about the effect you intend it to have.

> On the first day of every week, each one of you should set aside a sum of money in keeping with his income, saving it up, so that when I come no collections will have to be made. (1 Corinthians 16:2)

Give willingly

There are times when things are done grudgingly, out of a sense of duty or fear, or even guilt. Allow a spirit of 'wanting to give' to develop within you. This acknowledges the One who is the giver of all the good that we have in our possession.

> You may say to yourself, 'My power and the strength of my hands have produced this wealth for me.' But remember the Lord your God, for it is he who gives you the ability to produce wealth. (Deuteronomy 8:17–18)

Give totally

Sometimes there are opportunities to give ourselves as well as our resources – to develop closer ties with those we are giving to. This kind of giving is more costly than writing cheques, but it can often produce startling results. During the first century there were some communities that practised this kind of giving to an extraordinary degree.

> All the believers were one in heart and mind. No-one claimed that any of his possessions was his own, but they shared everything they had . . . There were no needy persons among them. For from time to time those who owned lands or houses sold them, brought the money from the sales and put it at the

apostles' feet, and it was distributed to anyone as he had need. (Acts 4:32,34–35)

To conclude, let's examine the following questions:

What are your savings goals?

- To provide for your family in some special way?
- To be able to support a good charitable cause?
- To release yourself to work for some good charitable cause?
- To ensure that your future will be secure?

Are there any responses you think you ought to try and change?

What are your giving patterns like?

Give yourself marks out of ten for the following:

- Proportionate
- Responsible
- Systematic
- Willing
- Total

Are there any changes you think you'd like to make here?

5.
For Richer, For Poorer?

Ingot we trust

That's not a misspelling. It is the philosophical slogan of millions of Christians and non-Christians alike. It's a slogan that firmly proclaims where the heart of twenty-first-century man truly lies. Our society is one that is focused on, if not actually driven by, the pursuit of wealth.

Life is about money – how to get it and how to keep it. At least that is how it's often portrayed, in magazine articles, radio and TV programmes, and so on. Is it true? Of all the chapters in this guide, this one is probably the most important because it addresses the basic beliefs people cherish in relation to money and wealth.

Everything in this chapter is structured around two fundamental questions. First, is it wrong to be rich? Among the world's super-rich there are people whose personal fortunes are greater than the wealth of entire nations. Is it wrong to be that rich? Is it wrong to *want* to be rich? Second, is it right to be poor? If prosperity is bad for us, might not poverty be good for us? Should we renounce the wealth culture, have as little to do with money as we can and try to live as frugally as possible?

What do you think? These are foundational issues, and what you feel about them is key. Your views, even beliefs, in this area will lead you to decide on the kind of game plan you will follow when it comes to things like balancing the family budget, spending, saving, charitable giving and larger matters, such as wealth creation and distribution. So, let's look at the options.

The case for being rich

Lots of good, public-spirited people are rich. Many churches, charities and good causes benefit from the generosity of rich people and rich institutions. Being rich doesn't necessarily equate with being selfish, mean-spirited, snobbish or uncaring.

Besides all this, 'rich' is a relative term, isn't it?

CASE STUDY

The Independent *asked a number of people, 'How rich is rich?' Of these, Ivan Mascow, a financial adviser, replied, 'Rich is when you can live off the interest of your capital. To live comfortably you'd need about £150,000 a year.' So you'd be rich if £150,000 is the interest on your capital. Quentin Crisp, well practised in living on very little, said, 'Everything is rich to me. I have nothing, I don't understand money. I'm happy as I am. If I had money I'd be full of anxiety.' Richard Platts, a Lloyds Name, said, 'I think £50,000 would be a rich man's salary. I've never had an income approaching even half of that, yet before I lost everything I regarded myself to be relatively well off. Now, at 60, I've nothing except my £12,000 pension and I've just received a bill from Lloyds' debt collectors demanding £800,000.' Hannah Moseley, unemployed, said, 'At the moment anyone who earns more than £7 an hour is rich. I consider really rich to be anyone who can do what they want to do and doesn't need to think about it.'* (*The Independent*, Sunday 9 October)

Parts of the Bible actually encourage and promote a wealth consciousness, as we have already noted. There is a widely held belief in some religious circles that money and wealth is a sign of divine approval, and a whole theology of prosperity has grown up around passages of Scripture such as the one referred to below. The message is multifaceted, but crudely stated it amounts to this: 'Love God, do as he says and you'll become rich and prosperous.' This religion of peace and prosperity is widely appealing; indeed it claims to have the backing and support of the very highest authority.

> If you pay attention to these laws and are careful to follow them, then the Lord your God will keep his covenant of love with you, as he swore to your forefathers. He will love you and bless you and increase your numbers. He will bless the fruit of your womb, the crops of your land – your grain, new wine and oil – the calves of your herds and the lambs of your flocks in the land that he swore to your forefathers to give you. You will be blessed more than any other people; none of your

> men or women will be childless, nor any of your livestock without young. The Lord will keep you free from every disease. (Deuteronomy 7:12–15)

Was the prodigal son in the parable Jesus told meant to be rich or poor (Luke 15:11–24)? What did his miserable state symbolise? The case is argued that prosperity is a tangible sign of God's blessing for those who are in a right relationship with their Father God. Poverty is a sign of his displeasure and it's something we bring upon ourselves, by and large.

But the concept is flawed. There are lots of good people in society who perform many charitable acts and lead exemplary lives, but they have not become prosperous as a result. Beyond this are others who serve God in quite open, explicit ways. They are clearly 'godly' in their lifestyles, their ambitions and their daily activities, but they do not all possess great wealth. Some, in fact, are penniless.

A half-truth is always more difficult to combat than a full-blown error, and it is a half-truth that presents itself to us here. It rests upon an important piece of biblical teaching, namely the great generosity and open-handedness of the Almighty towards his creation. But it is a distortion, because it takes one aspect of the Bible's teaching on money and wealth and turns it into the whole message. It ignores that other darker, potentially destructive, side of money that we are continually warned against.

> But if we have food and clothing, we will be content with that. People who want to get rich fall into temptation and a trap and into many foolish and harmful desires that plunge men into ruin and destruction. (1 Timothy 6:8–9)

The case for being poor

Poverty may be tough, but at least it's simple. Riches can be a snare and, strange as it may seem, they can hinder us from entering fully into life. Was this what Jesus meant when he declared that a camel could slip through the eye of a needle more easily than a wealthy man could enter the kingdom of God (Matthew 19:24)? The people listening to his words would have a vivid picture in their minds of a camel, heavily laden with goods, possessions and merchandise, struggling to pass through the narrow entrance into a walled town or city. It was a sight they must have often witnessed. Perhaps they'd watched with some amusement as the exasperated owner began to unburden his camel, compelled at last to acknowledge that there was no other way to get in!

Jesus was responding to a rich man who had asked him how he could have eternal life – a question that was more about the quality and essence of life than its duration. To this man he gave a staggering instruction: 'Go, sell your possessions and give to the poor, and you will have treasure in heaven. Then come, follow me' (Matthew 19:21).

We all want to enjoy those possessions whose value is non-negotiable: good relationships with others, activities that are meaningful and fulfilling, the beauty and wonder of the world. But all too often our view of money constrains us. There is an old saying, 'A man's soul is slightly smaller than his mortgage', and such a slightly smaller soul produces a certain meanness. Proverbs 11:24 tells us: 'One man gives freely, yet gains even more; another withholds unduly, but comes to poverty.'

The case for being poor is illustrated by the ancient

monastic vow of poverty, which was a direct response to the issue of money and its influence in a life. Intense renunciation was a way of saying 'no' to the values that prevailed in society. This response was not a knee-jerk reaction towards the times in which they lived. They were renouncing possessions in order to learn detachment. Poverty was not a penalty they had to suffer. They chose to be poor as a means to an end.

Sometimes the feeling that it's right to be poor stems not so much from renunciation as from resignation: a joyful acceptance, or a reluctance as the case may be, that poverty is the will of God.

> I find it interesting that the meanest life, the poorest existence, is attributed to God's will, but as human beings become more affluent, as their living standard and style begins to ascend the material scale, God descends the scale of responsibility at commensurate speed. (Maya Angelou, *I Know Why the Caged Bird Sings*)

There is an important distinction to be made between a positive acceptance of one's circumstances and a passive resignation towards them.

> I have learned to be content whatever the circumstances. I know what it is to be in need, and I know what it is to have plenty. I have learned the secret of being content in any and every situation, whether well fed or hungry, whether living in plenty or in want. (Philippians 4:11–12)

This brings us face to face with the issue suggested by the title of this chapter. Comparing the case for getting rich with that for becoming poor is almost bound to be inconclusive since in both cases there are 'things for' and 'things against'. There are moral principles at stake that ought to be taken into account, and personal circumstances also play their part.

For example, C.T. Studd, the famous nineteenth-century English cricketer, inherited a vast fortune, which he promptly used to fund his missionary work, much of which had quite explicit evangelical goals. On the other hand, the Cadbury brothers amassed great wealth through their entrepreneurship and business acumen. They saw themselves as wealth creators, providers of a product, and they chose to retain their wealth, using much of it to support philanthropic causes and promote social welfare.

Clearly, individual perceptions, preferences and priorities are all factors that have an influence. Nor should we forget that there is such a thing as the righteous acquisition of wealth and the righteous and generous disposition of it too.

> 'Give me neither poverty nor riches, but give me only my daily bread. Otherwise, I may have too much and disown you and say, "Who is the Lord?" Or I may become poor and steal, and so dishonour the name of my God.' (Proverbs 30:8–9)

Steering a course between two extremes is not necessarily the right way to go. People at the extremities of the wealth–poverty continuum often face uniquely challenging and stark choices when it comes to doing what they feel is right. The answer for them is not to move towards the mushy middle, but to stay as they are and face the challenge. But this is not easy, hence the wise man's plea for exemption in the proverb above.

What is right for you?

There are no tidy answers. But there are principles that can help us to chart our path. The first is the *concept of industry*. By this I mean applying yourself diligently to some worthwhile meaningful activity: 'Lazy hands make a man poor, but diligent hands bring wealth' (Proverbs 10:4). The Puritans were passionate about the sanctity of all honourable work, and in the process of working some of them became wealthy. But wealth was not their main preoccupation; it was a by-product of their industriousness. Their work was their calling; they saw it as an opportunity to glorify God and serve their neighbours. They also stressed the need to avoid overwork and scorned the mental attitude of the workaholic as much as they did laziness. Work was to them a way of honouring God rather than of making money, so too much work was as bad as too little. The Puritan writer Richard Steele warned that a person should not 'accumulate two or three callings to increase his riches'!

This Puritan model illustrates the value, even virtue, of being industrious, and shows it to be an important guideline where money and wealth are involved. The slothful and the lazy, those who find work dull and uninspiring, and the workaholics who take on two or three jobs to boost their income, should all take note. Rather than dispense with such a model as historic and out of date, we could benefit from allowing it to operate in our twenty-first-century lives.

The Puritan work ethic is missing from Western liberal democracies today. All the baggage that propelled people forward from the seventeenth century to industrial dominance during the twentieth has been stripped out, and in the process many have lost God as well. The pursuit of money distorts our view of life and work. Work becomes a quest for an extra few 'bucks' rather than something we do for vocational satisfaction or out of consideration for others. It's a quest that leaves broken and bruised people littering the path of success, whether from bankruptcy, stress or the overburden of making repayments brought about by credit that is too easy to obtain. We claim to use money, whereas in fact it's money that uses us! The guideline is clear: wholehearted, honest engagement in some worthwhile, meaningful work activity is one thing that will allow us to move forward with our lives without being focused on and driven by money.

Jesus told the parable of the talents in Matthew 25:14–30. A 'talent' was 6,000 small silver coins, each about the size of a 20p piece, worth in total around £1,000. One man was given five of these, another two, and a third just one. Each was given 'according to his ability'. There is a meritorious distinction between individuals which must be recognised. Some are more capable than others, and this virtually guarantees that societies will be unequal, though not necessarily unjust. The social dictum is 'to each according to their need, from each according to their ability'.

The three men were commissioned to trade, but only the first two made the effort. When the outcomes were reviewed, industry and an entrepreneurial spirit were commended; laziness and a lack of enterprise were roundly condemned. The point is well made.

A second principle emerges when we consider *our attitude to money*. Should we love it? Hate it? Fear it? The answer is: none of these. Rather, we should approach it with caution and recognise at the same time the possibilities it represents. This is what Jesus meant when he told a story about the manager of a family firm who was sacked for embezzlement (Luke 16:1–13). While he was still under notice, the manager called in a few of the firm's customers who still owed the firm money, amended the invoices they had been sent and explained to them that he was reducing their bills! He was smart. By this means he put them in his debt; they 'owed him one' and he could call in the favour when it suited him.

When the owner of the firm got to know the details, he was impressed by the manager's ingenuity and promptly reinstated his position. Without in any way condoning this man's behaviour, Jesus invites his disciples to learn from him and offers them this piece of advice: 'Use worldly wealth to gain friends'! We may take these cryptic words to mean 'recognise what possibilities money represents; use it, but don't let it use you'.

If money is used in the wrong way, it can destroy as few things can. But if you can conquer it and learn how to use it, its power is awesome. We see this wherever we look. Money can be used for non-economic purposes: it can be a weapon to bully people and keep them in check; it can be used to corrupt; it can be used to enlist the support of others. It is one of the greatest powers in human society.

Jesus is saying that money is to be captured, subdued and used for greater goals. If this principle is to operate in our lives, our attitude to money has to be that it is there to be used but not served. This is something that has to be learned and cultivated, but it takes a certain skill, an adroitness, to do it. Remember, money is not a neutral commodity; if we don't control it, it will control us.

If we wish to successfully employ a policy of using money without actually serving it, it helps if we understand its limitations. There are some things it cannot deliver. For example, material possessions cannot sustain or enhance the soul's well-being. This is what the rich farmer in the following parable either could not or would not grasp.

> 'The ground of a certain rich man produced a good crop. He thought to himself, "What shall I do? I have no place to store my crops."
>
> 'Then he said, "This is what I'll do. I will tear down my barns and build bigger ones, and there I will store all my grain and my goods. And I'll say to myself, 'You have plenty of good things laid up for many years. Take life easy; eat, drink and be merry.' "
>
> 'But God said to him, "You fool! This very night your life will be demanded from you. Then who will get what you have prepared for yourself?" ' (Luke 12:16–20)

He was running his business prudently, responsibly and with energy and foresight. His business plan was environmentally safe and socially acceptable, and he was not proposing to do anything illegal, immoral or harmful to his neighbours. Yet Jesus called him a fool. He was a fool because he was expecting that his material prosperity would feed through and benefit his soul. But it was impossible. He was a fool because his focus was wrong. He was serving money and expecting in return something that it would not and could not deliver. Material wealth cannot produce spiritual well-being. Only God can bring this about.

'Money can't buy happiness but at least you can choose your own kind of misery.' (Bob Hope)

Regard money as a vehicle, a means to an end. Don't let it become an all-powerful source on which you rely. Of course, just saying this doesn't make it happen. There are certain things we must do, and in the rough and tumble of life we shall soon discover that it is not easy to follow this principle. But we must continue to focus upon it – the more money is used rather than served, the more it will be a blessing instead of a curse.

A third guiding principle is *simplicity*. By this I mean having an uncomplicated, uncluttered, clear-sighted approach to money. One way to simplify your life is to have goals. These create clear perspectives by showing what is important and what isn't. Goals help you to concentrate on what matters and to avoid what doesn't. A goal is like a guiding star: it focuses your attention and gives you a sense of direction.

What are your goals in relation to money? Three things will help to ensure that your monetary goals are soundly based:

1. Pay close attention to what the Bible says and teaches about money, and let it govern your thinking.
2. Understand your personal feelings about money. Be clear about what they are and resolve any inconsistencies that may be present.
3. Consider the social angle. Think about the widening gap between the 'haves' and the 'have-nots'. Don't get bogged down in the arguments about what is causing it.

Just ask yourself whether there is something you can or should be doing about it and, if there is, resolve to do it.

The finest piece of advice ever given on these matters came from Jesus himself: 'Seek first [God's] kingdom and his righteousness, and all these things will be given to you as well' (Matthew 6:33). According to Jesus, the best way to simplify your life is to seek God. In the final analysis, simplicity equals trust.

6.
Wealth Creation and Distribution

'It was the best of times; it was the worst of times.' The famed opening stanzas of Charles Dickens' novel, *A Tale of Two Cities*, ring true today. For many it is indeed 'the best of times'. The life expectancy of the average UK citizen has increased by about 3.7 years. Inflation is now in single figures and likely to stay that way for the foreseeable future. Unemployment has been falling in recent years and most people can look forward to a reasonably healthy retirement. Of course, the unexpected sometimes happens and the longer term effects of the dreadful events that took place in New York in 2001 may yet cause all this to change.

But for others, this present day represents 'the worst of times'. Globalisation – it really is a small world these days – has led to greater industrialisation worldwide, which has generated huge amounts of wealth for some, but for many others it has produced extreme poverty.

This chapter is about wealth and the phenomenon of wealth creation. Where does the money come from? Who creates wealth and how do they do it? It is also about the vexing question of wealth distribution. Where does all the money go (although the question is not solely about the distribution of money – it includes lands and property as well)?

You may class yourself as a fairly average person with a moderate income, and wonder how wealth creation and its distribution can possibly be of concern to you. Surely these are global issues over which we have little or no influence. Isn't this a matter for governments and the big multi-national corporations?

Judged by worldwide standards, we who live in the West are wealthy. If you own a car or a home you are wealthier than over 90 per cent of the world's population. The fact that you've been able to afford the purchase of this book means that you are wealthy. The twin topics of wealth creation and wealth distribution *are* of concern to us, and raise matters that we should at least consider.

CASE STUDY

When I cycle here from the area in which I live, which takes about half an hour, it is with a sense of shame that I pass people who spent the night in shop doorways, are begging outside stations or spend their days wandering around the streets of London, hoping that someone will give them something to eat or something to do. None of that is necessary. The levels of wealth that exist in this country are obscene. I invite honourable mem-

bers, after we have finished our proceedings, to walk down to the back of the Savoy Hotel, where they would see a couple of hundred people sleeping on the pavement. Inside the hotel they would see people spending £50 per head on dinner. The obscenity of that kind of gap between the rich and the poor must be addressed.

On a global level the situation is worse. A quarter of the world's population live on the brink of starvation, while half live a very poor existence. In many African countries adult life expectancy is less than 50 years. In Russia, male life expectancy is currently falling to a similar level. In the coastal regions of Nigeria the exploitation of oil that has resulted from the harshness of the economic system has led to untold levels of brutality against the people.

My message is simply this. If we are to ensure that the planet survives this century and those that follow, we must deal with the gap between the rich and the poor – which leads to conflict and warfare – and environmental destruction. (Jeremy Corbyn, Debate on Wealth and Poverty in the Economic System. Hansard, Tuesday 16 May 2000)

Wealth has a meaning greater than money. Your wealth is the sum total of the things of value that you possess. Your house, car, jewellery, family heirlooms, treasured possessions and so on – as well as the money you have in the bank or building society or under the floorboards – these are the things that make up the tally of your wealth. There are of course, however, other possessions that on the face of it have no monetary value, yet we are rich because we have them: the love of a husband or wife, the loyalty and respect of friends, the support of family. Who could possibly calculate the worth of these?

Jesus told a parable in which he described the actions of a rich farmer (Luke 12:16–21). He spoke disparagingly of those who, like this farmer, created wealth for their own use, and concluded, 'This is how it will be with anyone who stores up things for himself but is not rich towards God' (verse 21).

Wealth creation

Three things happen when wealth is created:

1. A product is produced or a service is provided (e.g. a baker bakes bread; a cobbler repairs shoes; an accountant checks tax returns).
2. Value is added. The value of the product or service is greater at the point of sale than it was at the point of 'manufacture'.
3. An income is generated. This may go directly to the provider of the goods or services, or to the shareholder who put money into the business to enable it to function, or to people who are employed to help provide the goods or services.

CASE STUDY

A friend told me how his father got started in the fruit and veg business. He took his 'holiday' money from the carpet factory where he worked and, instead of using it to fund the usual week long family visit to the seaside that year, he went to the wholesaler's and bought a quantity of fruit and vegetables, came back to the town where he lived, set up a stall in the marketplace and discovered he could sell the products for more than he'd paid for them.

Twenty years later he had a large market stall, three shops in three different localities, a van specially fitted out to transport the large quantities of fruit, vegetables and flowers from the wholesaler's to each of his outlets, and fifteen employees, including his two sons, to help him run his business.

This fruit and veg man was a wealth creator. He provided a service that others wanted and were prepared to pay for. By virtue of what he did, he was also generating an income for himself and others who were helping him run his business.

We might ask why people don't go direct to wholesalers themselves or, better still, grow their own fruit and vegetables and flowers. Some actually do this, but the majority do not, maybe because they haven't got the time or the skill or the inclination. There is a market for the kind of product or service that the fruit and veg men provide, and it is a growing market!

Where, then, do people like us get the money we need to pay for the goods and services we require? Simple: most of us are part of other wealth-creating enterprises. We have an income from what we do. The fruit and veg man needs his shoes repaired, so he takes them to the cobbler's shop. Likewise the cobbler, or one of his employees, may need fruit and vegetables for his table, so he goes to the appropriate market stall or shop. There is a phenomenal degree of interaction and exchange going on in communities, across countries and between countries, and as a rule it is growing.

There is an index called the Gross Domestic Product (GDP) and it is used as a measure of the total of goods and services produced in one year by all the firms and companies that manufacture those goods and services in any particular country. GDP rises in more years than it falls, but every few years there is a pause or even a reduction in output. When GDP is increasing, this generally means the economy is growing and more wealth is being created. When it is decreasing, wealth is being eroded. On average the UK GDP grows at around 2.25 per cent each year.

Some people reading this will cry foul and say that these explanations are too simplistic and naïve, and that there is more to wealth creation than this. And indeed there is. But these are the small acorns from which the great oak trees of wealth creation and distribution, with all their variety and complexity, grow.

So who are the wealth creators? One of Terry Pratchett's novels, called *The Truth*, begins with a rumour that sweeps the countryside like wildfire, namely that dwarfs can turn lead into gold. When this rumour reaches the dwarfs themselves, it takes them by surprise, naturally, but they quickly see how this new reputation of theirs can be turned to advantage, and an ingenious plot develops.

Wealth creators, by definition, produce or help to produce a product or service that has added value in the marketplace and which generates an income for themselves and others. But not everyone who has an income is a wealth creator. There are those who accumulate wealth but do nothing to create it. The publishers of the book *Think and Grow Rich* were asked, 'Is the author himself a wealthy man?' They replied with wry good humour, 'He is from the sale of his books!' Some people will sell systems that may or may not work; the rest is up to the system user.

Others contribute only very indirectly to the wealth-creating processes. Indeed some seem not to create wealth at all by what they do and yet they play a part. For example, is a football star who earns £50,000 per week actually creating wealth by what he does? What about pop stars, comedians, entertainers? These all accumulate wealth, but do they create it? The answer is, by definition: yes they do! What about best selling novelists? Are they wealth creators? The well-known writer Catherine Cookson once described herself as 'an industry', and with some justification.

The wealth-creation process is going on all around us, in a variety of ways. Some people take from it but do not give to it. The parasite is an organism that depends on its host for support, but it gives nothing in return. It is totally selfish and does not contribute to sustaining the ecosystem. It is important that those with a Christian worldview shun the principle of parasitism and seek instead a role that enriches and adds value within the society of which they are part. The first teachers of the Christian gospel exemplified this by the way they lived and, as a rule, Christians ought to be wealth creators *par excellence*.

> I have not coveted anyone's silver or gold or clothing. You yourselves know that these hands of mine have supplied my own needs and the needs of my companions. In everything I did, I showed you that by this kind of hard work we must help the weak, remembering the words the Lord Jesus himself said: 'It is more blessed to give than to receive.' (Acts 20:33–35)

It is not enough simply to create wealth; it is the righteous creation or acquisition of wealth that matters.

> Like a partridge that hatches eggs it did not lay is the man who gains riches by unjust means. When his life is half gone,

they will desert him, and in the end he will prove to be a fool. (Jeremiah 17:11)

Think about some of the ways in which wealth is acquired by unrighteous means:

1. People become rich by *illegal* means, e.g. certain aspects of the arms trade, drug dealing, prostitution, pornography. These represent multimillion pound businesses.
2. People become rich by *unjust* means, e.g. the exploitation of labour, particularly child labour in some countries.
3. People become rich by *uncaring* means, e.g. the so-called 'asset strippers' who buy an ailing business (a wealth-creating facility no less), sell off the profitable bits and close the remainder, destroying many valuable jobs in the process.
4. People become rich by *dishonest* means, e.g. fraudulent dealing, as in selling shoddy or faulty goods and charging the customer as though they were top quality or in perfect condition. There is also embezzlement, where you take something that is not yours and use it as though it were. The notorious case involving a well-known businessman who raided his company's pension funds for his own ends and cheated others out of what was rightfully theirs is an example of this.

Thus there are ways of becoming wealthy or of simply acquiring money, be it on a small or large scale, that are not right. This applies to individuals as much as to large corporations and governments.

There are two basic ways of acquiring wealth. One is to

inherit it and the other is to create it – which implies more than earning it. The parable of the talents is about the creation of wealth. The man who is given five talents makes them into ten. We are not told how – maybe he got a nice little business going, which generated incomes for others. We must assume that whatever was done was done legitimately, fairly, honestly and with due regard for the rights and welfare of others. Likewise, the man who was given two talents made them into four. The third man did nothing and it is clear from the teaching of the parable that doing nothing is not an option. Wealth creation is here to stay; it is a necessary part of our economic structures. It will go on happening, one way or another. This makes the need to create wealth *righteously* all the more pressing in view of our social, community and spiritual well-being.

Wealth distribution

Now let's look at the other side of the coin (if you'll pardon the pun!): namely, wealth distribution. The distribution of wealth within a society is as crucial as its creation. A society that allows the rich within it to get richer while the poor become poorer is really a society divided against itself, and one that cannot, in the long run, be sustained. The social and economic volatility caused by this perceived inequality can create pressures that are difficult to contain. Severe disruption and even the breakdown of key structures and institutions often occur: witness the events that led to the French Revolution during the eighteenth century; the overthrow of the Russian tsar in 1915 and the rise of Communism in that great country; the emergence of the Chinese People's Republic in 1948 and so on. We do well to remember that these climactic events were spawned by economic as well as political forces, and wealth distribution was one of the core issues. We in the West need to keep a close watch on what is happening within our own societies as the gap between rich and poor continues to grow steadily.

But it is not simply the social and economic implications of wealth distribution that make this topic significant. There are moral implications too and it is the righteous distribution of wealth that is the primary concern of this section.

Question: Can we afford to let the wealth creators take care of this issue?

We should not discount this notion. There have been, and still are, many great benefactors of society – wealthy men and women who have worked tirelessly for the good of others and who have used their wealth to bring about improvements in the general standard of living of the masses.

The Bible speaks against a selfish, hoarding spirit and favours a generous, wealth-distributing attitude: 'Do not withhold good from those who deserve it, when it is in your power to act' (Proverbs 3:27). This means more than just giving to those in need; it implies a righteous deployment of wealth towards those who are entitled to it, and includes matters like paying bills on time, settling accounts in full, paying fees, wages and salaries that are fitting for the work undertaken. It excludes making unfair or unjust demands for money or a share of business rewards.

Question: Can we afford to let governments take care of this issue?

Arguably it is governments that have the greatest influence over wealth distribution. Governments can pass laws that limit trade; they can provide subsidies that enliven trade; they can levy taxes that enable a redistribution of wealth to take place. But too much government interference can be counterproductive. Many of the big players in the wealth-creation league opt out of this role, as governments increasingly take over the responsibility of ensuring fair and equable distribution of wealth. In the United States, where the burden of taxation is low compared with other countries, the per capita level of charitable giving, both corporate and private, is said to be among the highest in the world. Some observers see a correlation between these two: high levels of taxation lead to lower levels of giving and fewer benefactors, since the latter will increasingly see the government as taking on the job of welfare and wealth distribution for the benefit of the less well off.

Question: Can we afford to let the market take care of this issue?

Sir Eddie George, Governor of the Bank of England, once remarked: 'I have a firm belief in markets. I don't believe they are always perfect, but by and large, if they get it wrong, they put it right faster than administration or bureaucrats could.' Does that apply to the distribution of wealth? Can we rely on market forces to ensure a fair, if not equal, distribution? Market forces can compel governments to alter course. But markets can also be manipulated: by reducing or increasing the flow of crude oil to the free world; by creating butter mountains and wine lakes in Europe; by stockpiling grain in the USA. Throttling back on or regulating the supply of commodities to the marketplace by artificial means pushes demand upwards and, with it, supplier revenues.

The fact is that no single institution or group of individuals could guarantee the righteous distribution of wealth, even if they wanted to. There is no system, economic or otherwise, that can do it either. But each of these may play a part and can exert a positive as well as a negative influence. However, it is the Scriptures that contain the greatest number of clues to the means of distributing wealth righteously. Take, for example, land and property. The Old Testament (Leviticus 25) sets out the special terms under which land and property could be bought, sold and used. Land could not be sold outright because it was deemed to belong to God, and people were allowed only the use of it. Every seventh year was declared a year of rest for the land, during which its cultivation was forbidden.

Every fiftieth year, called the Year of Jubilee, an estate that had been sold had to be restored to its original owners or their descendants. The repurchase price was fixed according to the number of production years remaining until the next year of restoration. If, meanwhile, an Israeli became poor and was forced to sell his land, his closest relative, or himself if he again became prosperous enough, had to have the opportunity of repurchasing the land at a price equivalent to the crop yield remaining until the next year of restoration. Whoever sold a house in a walled city had the right to buy it back, but only during the first full year from the date of sale.

Clearly this system favoured land users rather than land

owners – you benefited only if you used the land, not if you owned it. Land consists of the earth and the soil and everything provided by nature before human labour is applied to it. Raw materials can be mined from it, animals can be tamed and domesticated, and plants can be harvested for food, clothing, shelter and industry. These things could be held as property because there is a natural right to the product of one's own labour. The land itself could not be owned by right of work, but only to the extent of right of title created by law. This maintained a balance in the wealth distribution stakes and prevented profiteering.

Today, increases in land value are determined by location and the presence or activity of the community around it. Effectively this amounts to a 'betterment' value and it is clearly possible for a speculator to buy land, wait until the price rises, then resell at a profit. A possible way of introducing a modern equivalent of the ancient Levitical system would be to implement a land value tax, based on 'betterment' values, for public benefit.

There is hardly anything clearer in the Bible than the concept of God's ownership of everything: 'The earth is the Lord's, and everything in it, the world, and all who live in it' (Psalm 24:1). As absolute owner, God puts limits on the rights of individuals to accumulate wealth. For instance, a percentage of the produce of the God-given Promised Land was to be handed to the poor, according to Moses (Deuteronomy 14:28–29). Every fiftieth year was to be a 'jubilee' year in which all slaves were set free, all debts were cancelled and the land was returned to its origins. The divine rationale for upsetting everyone's economic applecarts was simply 'the land is mine' (Leviticus 25:23). This concept of God as owner and ourselves as stewards permeates the Scriptures and ought to permeate the wealth-creation and wealth-distribution debate among Christians too.

This leads to another important consideration: the poor. Jesus made lots of observations about the poor in society, but his comment about the fact that there will always be people who are poor (Matthew 26:11) has proved true. Poverty has been defined as 'families who live on less than half the average national income'. This means that throughout the world, including the developed countries, one in every three children lives in poverty. One of the tests of the moral basis of any society lies in asking the question, 'What does it do for the poor?'

Jesus did not envisage a society that was equal in terms of the wealth of its individual members. That does not mean that we should cease working for a more equal society, but we should recognise that equality implies equality of justice, opportunity, fair play and human treatment, and not just equality of wealth. What can we do?

Do the poor always have to be the same 'poor'? There is much that can be done to create opportunities for the poor to move out of the poverty trap. It is to the credit of people with deeply held religious convictions that many of them have been at the forefront of initiatives designed to do this. It is often truthfully remarked that the establishment of the welfare state in Great Britain owes more to the influence of Methodism than Marxism.

The old maxim 'give a man a fish and you feed him for a day; teach him how to fish and you feed him for a lifetime' rings especially true. Benevolent funds, scholarships and legacies large and small, bequeathed by individuals, can all be used to create opportunities for the poor alongside organisations and governments with a philanthropic bias, and are a reflection of the Spirit of Christ among us. Wealth creation and wealth distribution are key elements affecting the way communities and whole societies function today, but it is the *righteous* dimension, whether operating or lacking, that constitutes the springboard for Christian action.

7.

Money and Morals

Having money means having power, but what should we do with this money power? More to the point, perhaps, is the question, 'What might this money power do with us?'

Ethics, by which is meant 'the moral quality of a course of action', has become a popular topic in many business schools in the UK and the USA. This sounds fine until you realise that ethics can be, and often is, taught in two quite separate ways. It can be taught using the model of absolute values or, as some theologians and philosophers put it, 'first principles'. Or it can be taught in terms of how we all have our own way of seeing things, using the idea that values are relative to each person and the situations they find themselves in. Money is the perfect example of this.

Money is more than a medium of exchange. It is the liquid form of wealth. You can freeze your money to turn it into possessions. You can boil it up to turn it into different kinds of power, such as using it to impress your friends or cherish your loved ones. And you can use it to guard against a 'rainy day'. It is like a cushion or a wall – it seems to offer security, health and a sense of well-being. With money in your pocket you're prepared for the day-to-day eventualities that often crop up without too much warning. With money in the bank, the world can seem a kinder place.

Let's face it, money can be a blessing and we must not lose sight of the good that can come about through its proper use. It is crystal clear that our society knows how to put money to good use. You only have to think about some of the results of the Children in Need appeals, and other less publicised but equally worthy fundraising efforts, to realise this.

But money can be a curse as well as a cure and we readily acknowledge that affluence has a downside. We are less eager, perhaps, to admit to the potentially destructive and corrupting influence of money and wealth, and to the detrimental effects it may be having on our souls.

CASE STUDY

John Paul Getty, the oil magnate, lived to make money. He became the richest man in the world, the most successful businessman of his generation. It has been estimated that the average person would have to win the lottery, big time, every day for 800 years to become as rich as he was! Getty's father, himself a millionaire, was a devout Christian. He was so concerned about his son's obsession with money that he cut him out of his will, but to no avail – Getty went on to make his own fortune. He was not the happiest of men, however, and it is said that his obsession with money destroyed him as a person and wrought havoc within his family.

It is of singular note that one of his sons from one of his five failed marriages, having recovered from a heroin addiction, has given away most of his share of his father's millions. He is one of the world's greatest benefactors and, unlike his father, is said to be a man at peace with himself.

To Jesus' question 'What good will it be for a man if he gains the whole world, yet forfeits his soul?' (Matthew 16:26) the market offers a graded answer, as the following suggests:

> First man: 'What profit is there for a man who gains the whole world but loses his soul?'
>
> Second man: 'Well, we've done a few figures on this and . . . you might be pleasantly surprised because it seems that there is *quite* a profit, quite a *nice* profit in fact.'
>
> First man: 'And what would the profit be like if you lost, say, half your soul?'
>
> Second man: 'Still very nice. It's a huge audience – a huge market – and I'd like you to consider the following. I know a man who has only one *sixteenth* of his soul left and he's happy – perfectly happy!' (Michael Leunig, *Sydney Morning Post*)

Desiring money and wealth and despising money and wealth are plainly shown as being opposite ends of the biblical spectrum, and we should avoid migrating towards either one. In the parable of the shrewd manager (Luke 16:1–13), already referred to in Chapter 5, Jesus opens up the moral question and provides us with a practical stratagem for dealing with money without getting our hands dirty in the process. He urges his followers to make friends by making use of worldly wealth (Luke 16:9). But he concludes his application of the teaching by saying, 'You cannot serve both God and Money' (verse 13). Money is contrasted with God, implying that it is something that can be served, even worshipped – something that is fully capable of getting hold of its users and exerting an influence upon them and their actions.

Christ acknowledges the place that money and wealth have in our world. It is clearly an integral and indispensable part of the world system. Followers of Christ, though not 'of the world', are certainly *in* it and therefore have to deal, among other things, with money. But it is *how* they deal with it that is shown to be so crucial. The teaching of the parable is clear: they are to use it, not serve it. They are not to elevate it to the place where it is revered as the panacea of all ills, the golden key that will unlock any situation, the solution to every problem. They are to be proactive users of money, not its reactive servants.

Having told this parable, Jesus chides his followers over their naïvety and lack of creative action. The shrewd manager is shown to have used economic means for non-economic ends. He was not driven by the god Mammon to devise a get-rich-quick scheme or develop a money-making concern. He used the facility of money to serve a higher purpose – in this case his future personal well-being. 'The master commended the dishonest manager because he had acted shrewdly. For the people of this world are more shrewd in dealing with their own kind than are the people of the light' (Luke 16:8).

This is really a parable of Christian prudence. The followers of Christ are to use the world's goods against the world and for God. Joseph of Arimathea and Nicodemus were both rich men. Although prominent members of the Jewish religious council of their day, they were also secret disciples of Christ. After Jesus was crucified they went to the Roman governor, Pontius Pilate, and begged him to release the body to them. He consented to this, but did they have to part with money to get him to do it? The Bible narrative doesn't say, but if the payment of money had been requisite would they have paid? The answer is probably 'yes'. Jesus was buried in a very expensive tomb, provided by the same Joseph of Arimathea. The spices and other aromatic substances used to prepare his body for burial were supplied by Joseph and Nicodemus, at considerable cost. Jesus and his disciples used money to meet their daily needs and facilitate their ministry, and down through the centuries since then other followers of Christ have done similar things – raised money and used wealth to further the purposes of the kingdom of God. There is an art to spending money as well as earning it.

Using money without serving it is easier said than done. What begins from the best of motives can end as egg all over the proverbial face.

CASE STUDY

Paul Flynn, Member of Parliament for Newport West, asked Michael Alison, representing the Church of England Church Commissioners, 'When will the Commissioners deal with their investment in the international arms trade?' (In 1994 the Church Commissioners had 2,700,000 shares in GEC valued at £1,772,000.) Alison replied, 'We are investors in GEC, whose armaments portfolio is held to be less than 30 per cent, which is the cut-off point for our ethical applications.'

Paul Flynn then issued a press release 'on behalf of the Archbishop of Canterbury':

> *In its report today the Archbishop's working party on sin proposes a radical new approach. In future, it suggests, sin should be defined as 'immoral behaviour in which a person engages for not less than 30% of the time'.*
>
> *Commenting favourably on the report, the Archbishop said, 'Our approach to sin has always been subject to ethical criteria which are constantly under review. We need a practical definition based on the realities of modern life. Nevertheless, the Church does not approve of those whose main business is sin. A cut-off point of 30% is realistic.'*

Despite the difficulties, there are several positive steps we can take that will lead us away from serving money, and towards using it:

1. *Get a biblical perspective on it.* Read all you can about this, the second most recurring theme in the Scriptures. Let the Bible's truth about money grip your mind.
2. *Dethrone it.* Without doubt, money has assumed an almost sacred character in our world. It is too high on our list of values, and we must dethrone it. One of the finest ways to do this is to give it away. Next time you monitor a spirit of covetousness within your heart, crucify it by the simple act of giving. This will break the power of money.
3. *Manage it.* Budget your money. Plan how you are going

to use it. Start with giving. Control your spending, be sensitive to the needs of others round you. Control and manage your money to the glory of God and for the good of others.

4. *Pray over it.* Pray over how to budget your money. Pray for freedom from money's power. Pray that Christians in business will control, invest and channel money in creative, life-enhancing ways. Pray that governments will divert their vast resources from making bombs to, say, making bread. Pray for wisdom where there are financial problems and for protection for those who are doing well, and if they have to control and use money that they will be free from avarice.

Money has to be conquered and converted to the way of Christ. Then it can be used without being served.

8.
Loose Change

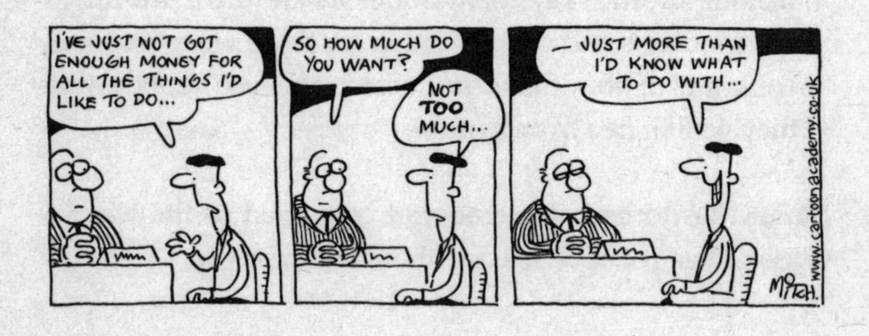

The symbol of Britain's national wealth today is a small gold-coloured coin weighing just nine and a half grams and made from a mixture of copper, nickel and zinc. It is produced by the Royal Mint at Llantrisant in South Wales on some of the most advanced casting machinery in the world. It is the pound sterling and it no longer counts for very much. Its intrinsic value is negligible and it has a purchasing power to match; it will not even buy you the cheapest fare on the London Underground. Just another coin to rattle in your pocket. At the last count there were a billion pound coins in circulation, which means that in theory at least, every man, woman and child in Britain has about eighteen of them stashed away somewhere!

The very first pound coin was minted in 1489 by King

Henry VII. Since then it has taken many different forms, surviving the rigours of war and peace and political mergers to the present day. The pound has had a good run for its money, but its long and unique history will soon come to an end, for there's a new kid on the block – the Euro.

Some people would like to preserve the pound as a symbol of Britain's financial heritage and national pride. There are sentimental, psychological and, some would say, sound economic reasons for keeping the pound. Others say it has outlived its usefulness and should be replaced. Some would even claim that we now live in a society that does not have a pressing need for real money at all. If so, the pound will have to go, as part of a general abandonment of what we learned to call currency.

But it is not the pound that matters or, come to that, the Euro or the dollar. It is what it represents:

- a medium of exchange;
- a means to power and influence;
- Mammon – the money god.

This makes the issue a deeper and more personal one. There are those who want to collect coins, lots of them, and hoard them. Others – philanthropic, fair-minded souls – want to share them with those who appear to need them. Most of us simply want to use our money as a means of exchange so that we can have the things we want or need.

This book has been about the choices and decisions that confront people who want to live principled as well as profitable lives in this area. It has aimed at identifying and helping you to understand the major issues. Here, in this chapter, the key themes are drawn together and summarised to guide you in developing practical life strategies for doing things with your money in ways that reflect Christian values.

These key themes are:

- Learn about money.
- Get in touch with your feelings about money.
- Resolve to live simply.
- Know how much you are worth.
- Set financial goals.
- Start budgeting.
- Learn how to use money.

Learn about money

Money is not complicated. The principles behind financial transactions are simple enough, and there's no need for you to become a financial whizz-kid. It is enough that you understand certain basic things, such as:

- how money works, i.e. how it flows, how it is generated, how it loses and gains value;
- the difference between capital and income;
- the difference between saving and investing;
- what wealth is – how it is created and how it is distributed.

Next, there's the psychological side. We must appreciate ,

- the importance and significance of money within our society;
- the power of money and how it can be used to regulate

the behaviour of individuals and whole communities, and how it can rule behaviour in an oppressive sense.

Finally, there is the spiritual side, and it is vital that we are aware of

- the fascination that money has and the destructive as well as positive results it can produce in people and groups and within organisations;
- the fact that money is a power in its own right.

Get in touch with your feelings about money

Remembering that money is a medium of exchange, you could ask, 'What do I need to exchange it for?' Is it a need or a want? Consider the following before making a purchase:

- Do I need this or merely want it?
- Do I have the money to pay for it?
- How will this affect me spiritually?
- How much will this cost each time I use it?
- Is there anyone I could or should talk to before buying this, who would give me a neutral opinion?
- How much will this item depreciate in future months and years? What's the real long-term cost?
- Am I paying for features I don't really need?

Clearly these questions may not all apply in each and every case, but it's a useful list that will help you to run the rule over anything you are thinking of acquiring in exchange for money.

Getting in touch with how you feel about money also

means remembering that it is a means to power and can be used to influence people and situations. How do you feel about this? You may think that you do not have enough money to influence others to any great extent, but do you allow yourself to be influenced by people who do, or by the prospect of obtaining money for yourself through them?

Money is Mammon – the money god. How do you cope with this concept? Do you regard it as a fantasy or a reality? Examine your own heart – are you in pursuit of riches? Do you love money? Or is poverty your goal, because you fear money? Do you claim neutrality, prepared simply to accept whatever comes your way (and secretly hope it's wealth!)?

Resolve to live simply

Instead of vowing prosperity or poverty, vow simplicity.

> So do not worry, saying, 'What shall we eat?' or 'What shall we drink?' or 'What shall we wear?' For the pagans run after all these things, and your heavenly Father knows that you need them. But seek first his kingdom and his righteousness, and all these things will be given to you as well. Therefore do not worry about tomorrow, for tomorrow will worry about itself. Each day has enough trouble of its own. (Matthew 6:31–34)

Here's a checklist that will help you work through what this means in practical terms:

- Buy things for their usefulness, not their status.
- Reject anything that is producing an addiction in you.
- Get into the habit of giving things away.
- Resist advertisements that persuade you to buy things you don't really need.

- Get into the way of enjoying things without having to own them.

Know how much you are worth

It's important to keep a check on this. Knowing what you are worth will help you enormously when it comes to making decisions about wealth and money, e.g. when spending, budgeting, saving or giving. If you don't know how much you are worth, you won't know what you can afford and you may find yourself running into debt without realising, or borrowing money when you don't need to.

A simple way of keeping up to date with what you are worth is to produce a table like the one below. List all the things you own that have monetary value – your assets. Alongside this make a list of all the things on which you owe something – your liabilities. Add up your assets and your liabilities, subtract one from the other and this will give you your net worth.

ASSET	VALUE (£)	LIABILITY	AMOUNT (£)
House	60,000	Mortgage	23,500
Car	4,000	Credit cards	5,000
Life insurance	20,000	Bank loan	2,000
Jewellery	1,500	Hire purchase a/c	550
Savings account	500		
Furnishings	2,500		
Stamp collection	650		
TOTALS	**89,150**		**31,050**

Net worth = £58,100 (£89,150 – £31,050)

Knowing what you are worth leads to the next step.

Set financial goals

Remember the three basic things we can do with money: spend it, accumulate it and give it away. It makes good sense to set financial targets in each of these areas. Many people are spenders only, but we should set a giving goal and a savings goal too. You'll be surprised at what this will lead to and at how well you are able to rise to the challenge. You may begin by thinking that the only way to achieve your goals is to have more income, but you may also discover that you can reduce your spending in some areas. Don't be depressed if the picture seems to be one of mounting debts, and your only strategy appears to be that of making ends meet. Take a moment to recall the old cliché, 'Man's extremity is God's opportunity', as it's true! Often, in times of deep adversity and straitened circumstances, the stimulus and creativity of the God within can be at its strongest, and if we put God first, by giving, we will almost certainly find other things dropping into place.

'Sometimes it is necessary to hear a negative message before anything positive can begin.' (Sören Kierkegaard)

Start budgeting

If you haven't started doing this yet, resolve to start now – even if it only serves to highlight the difficulties you face. But most likely it will highlight the solutions at the same time. Budgeting enables you to see the obstacles before you have to deal with them; it helps you to develop sensible financial plans. These needn't involve highly complex investment strategies. They may be just plain, straightforward calculations involving relatively small amounts of money. But budgeting will help you keep track of your funds, plan your way out of debt, guide your spending decisions, assist the timing of your actions and generally put you in control of your finances.

Learn how to use money

This is possibly the area in which we have most to learn. The secret is not to deny money its place in your life. Learn to acknowledge the fact of it, the necessity and even the power of it, without becoming dependent upon it. Don't despise its use, but don't rely on it either. Become the kind of person who uses money without serving it.

EPILOGUE

Rich Man, Poor Man . . .

George Oliver Digby, known to friends and enemies alike simply as 'Digby', was at a banquet. A banquet given in his honour of course. His was a household name in Silica Dale, the town where he lived. He owned a sizeable chunk of it too and rumour had it that he was its richest inhabitant. He was draining his second cup of coffee when the public address system crackled into life. Suddenly, above the clatter of dishes and cutlery, a voice boomed, 'Ladies and gentlemen, may I have your attention please? I have an announcement to make.'

Digby looked up and saw the speaker, a slight, shabbily dressed figure. A hush settled over the room, then the little man drew a breath, looked straight at the microphone and said, 'The richest man in Silica Dale will die at twelve o'clock tonight!'

Shocked silence. Then pandemonium broke loose, everyone talking at once. Then another hush, and now everyone was staring at Digby. Angrily he snatched the napkin from under his chin and lurched unsteadily to his feet. 'What are you all staring at, you fools?' he roared. 'Is this some kind of joke? I'm not the one. It's not me . . . I'm not . . .'

That was when he woke up! Little beads of sweat clung to his forehead and his breath came in gasps. A dream, a silly dream, that was all. He clutched at the bedside clock; it showed the time was four in the morning. He shook his head, settled back onto the pillows and tried not to go back to sleep again.

Later, a gentle double tap on the door awoke him. It was the butler, bearing the usual silver tray with Digby's breakfast. But Digby waved it away. He couldn't face it.

He lay for a while wondering what to do, then abruptly he got out of bed, dressed and rang for the butler. 'Ring the office,' he said. 'Tell them not to expect me. I'm having the day off. Then have the car brought round in half an hour.'

'Very good, sir,' said the butler smoothly. 'And will you require the services of Brown, the chauffeur, sir?'

'No, I'll drive myself.'

'Ah, that's good, sir. Perhaps I could just mention . . .'

Digby cut him short. 'Not now,' he snapped. 'I'm short of time as it is.'

Digby steered the gleaming Rolls through the town and parked outside a building discreetly marked 'Private Surgery'. Inside, he announced that he wanted 'a complete check up – heart, lungs, the lot'.

The examination concluded with the doctor's pronouncement that Digby had 'nothing wrong with him and would likely live for ever'.

'No chance of me, er, dropping dead suddenly then, Doc?' Digby gave an embarrassed little laugh.

'No reason,' said the doctor. 'Why? What's bothering you?'

'Nothing,' said Digby breezily. 'Nothing at all.'

Next stop was the local police station. Seated in front of

the station superintendent, Digby listened impatiently as the 'super' explained that he couldn't possibly send any men to patrol Digby's mansion that night.

'I'm sure you're in no danger, Digby old son,' he said, 'but if you're so worried, there are plenty of private security firms around that you could hire to do what you want.'

Outside the police station Digby decided there was one more call he must make. There was one person who would know for sure whether he was the richest man in Silica Dale.

His bank manager was cagey about the request at first. 'It depends what you mean by "rich", Mr Digby,' he said evenly.

'What are you talking about?' Digby snorted. 'We all know what being rich means. It means having money, lots of it! So just tell me! Go on, tell me . . .'

The bank manager nodded slowly. 'In that case,' he said, 'there's no doubt about it – no doubt at all.' Digby waited, tense. 'You are,' the manager went on, 'without question, the richest man in Silica Dale.'

'No!' groaned Digby. 'Are you sure there's no one else just a teeny bit richer than me?'

'Quite sure,' said the bank manager. 'Why? Is that a problem?'

'Don't ask,' growled Digby, and left.

It was almost lunchtime, but Digby skipped it and went home. He rang for his butler. 'I want to talk to a minister – a good one,' he said.

'You're in luck, sir,' smiled the butler. 'The Reverend Toogood is here now. He's very good.'

'What's a minister doing here?' said Digby.

'He's visiting Brown, your chauffeur. I tried to tell you

about Brown earlier, sir. He's . . .'

'Yes, yes,' said Digby, 'never mind that now. Just get this Reverend Topside . . .'

'Thank you for sparing me some of your valuable time, Reverend,' Digby greeted the Reverend Toogood politely.

'It's no trouble at all, Mr Digby,' the clergyman explained. 'I was here anyway, visiting your chauffeur, Brown. As you know, he's been taken ill recently.'

'Yes, I knew that,' Digby lied.

'He's your gardener too and general handyman, isn't he? A good worker, I'm sure of that, and a faithful member of our congregation. A most loving, godly man.'

Digby shifted uncomfortably. 'Listen, Reverend, er, Hopgood, I've had this dream and it's been bothering me. I wonder if you could explain it?'

The Reverend Toogood listened patiently while Digby talked. 'I'm sorry you're so upset, Mr Digby. There's really no need.'

'No?' said Digby eagerly.

'No. Take your chauffeur as an example.'

'I'd rather not, Reverend Hopside. I was hoping you could explain this dream for me.'

'Well, OK Digby. Let's begin by exploring this fear you have of death.'

'What are you talking about?' said Digby indignantly. 'I'm not afraid of dying. I just don't want to – not yet, anyway. I've too many things to live for.'

'What things?' said the clergyman quietly.

Digby began compiling a list of things he thought he'd mention, then decided against all of them. He didn't want to appear selfish.

'You know, Mr Digby,' the Reverend went on, 'people

who live mostly for themselves are often lonely, even unhappy.'

That did it! Digby waved the Reverend Toogood away. He'd heard enough.

He spent the rest of the day trying to take his mind off the dream, but the words of the little man kept going round in his head: 'The richest man in Silica Dale will die at twelve o'clock tonight!' He played snooker. He drank a lot. He watched a film on TV – until one of the main characters, a middle-aged millionaire, died suddenly of a heart attack. Digby switched off.

'Excuse me, sir.' It was the butler. 'The security firm whose services you engaged today have arrived. I'm to tell you, sir, that the, er, bodyguards are patrolling the grounds now, with their dogs.'

Digby nodded. 'Good,' he said, then added, 'I'm not going to bed tonight, so leave all the lights on in the house.'

He sat in his armchair and watched the clock. It reached the hour of midnight and began to strike. Digby waited, beads of sweat gathering on his forehead, his heart pounding. The clock finished striking twelve; then stillness. Everything seemed normal. Digby felt normal. He laughed to himself. What a fool he'd been; what a waste of the day. He got up and paced the room. Five past twelve now and he was beginning to feel hungry. 'Kitchen,' he thought. 'A nice snack from the fridge.' He made for the door, and suddenly stopped. There was a gentle tap, and slowly it began to open. He stared at it, open-mouthed.

The butler appeared, framed in the doorway. 'Sorry to disturb you, sir,' he murmured. 'We knew you'd still be awake and thought you ought to know right away.'

'Know what?' croaked Digby.

'Brown the chauffeur, sir. He's not been well recently. We tried to tell you earlier, but you've been busy.'

'What about Brown?'

'He's . . . dead, sir.'

'Really?' said Digby weakly. 'When was this?'

'Just a short while ago, sir – right on the stroke of midnight. Thought you'd like to know.'

Brown: overworked, underpaid, undervalued Brown; God-fearing, churchgoing Brown. Could it be that the richest man in Silica Dale really had died at twelve o'clock that night after all?

Perhaps the most disturbing text on wealth in the entire canon of Scripture is where those who say, 'I am rich; I have acquired wealth and do not need a thing,' are described as 'wretched, pitiful, poor, blind and naked'. They are told to 'buy . . . gold refined in the fire' so that they can remedy their situation (Revelation 3:17–18).

The figurative use of the ideas of poverty and riches in this text is meant to signify two things. First, those who are materially rich may not be rich at all, and second, true riches may not be within their budget. The command to 'buy . . . fine gold refined in the fire' is like the description of the rich as being poor; those who think they are rich will discover that they are not and those who think they can access this essential wealth will find that they cannot.

The road to riches begins when (like Digby perhaps) we are brought to acknowledge our spiritual bankruptcy and accept Christ's offer of a personal relationship and friendship:

'Here I am! I stand at the door and knock. If anyone hears my voice and opens the door, I will come in and eat with him, and he with me.' (Revelation 3:20)

Bibliography

Cohen, Bernice, *The Money Maze* (Orion Business Books, 1998).

Foster, Richard J., *Money, Sex and Power* (Hodder and Stoughton, 1985).

House of Commons Hansard Debates, *Wealth and Poverty in the Economic System*, 16 May 2000.

Rowe, Dorothy, *The Real Meaning of Money* (HarperCollins, 1997).

Sinclair, David, *The Pound, a Biography* (Century, 2000).

Shortcuts

A fast route to this guide's themes

Other LifeGuides include . . .

Battle for the Mind
by David Holden

Practical and down to earth, this book will show you how to face the daily onslaught in your thought life and how to renew your mind. It really is possible!

Keep on Running
by Sue Barnett

With down to earth practicality and humour, popular speaker and author Sue Barnett shares the highs and lows of marathon running, closely relating them to the spiritual side of the 'human race'.

No Sex Please, We're Single
by Ian Gregory

More Christians are staying single for longer despite not wanting to. Ian Gregory examines why involuntary singleness is on the rise. He offers ideas on how to improve your chances of meeting someone right for you. And he challenges churches to rethink the way they treat singles. For singleness is not just a personal issue, but affects the growth and wellbeing of the church as a whole.